>revolution
DEVOTIONAL

D0957453

90 DAILY DEVOTIONS FOR GUYS

>> Revolution Devotional

Randy Southern and Chris Hudson

ZONDERVAN™
RAND RAPIDS, MICHIGAN 49530 USA

ZONDERVAN.COM/
AUTHORTRACKER

Youth Specialties
www.youthspecialties.com

Youth Specialties

Revolution Devotional
Copyright © 2005 by The Livingstone Corporation

Youth Specialties products, 300 South Pierce Street, El Cajon, CA 92020, are published
by Zondervan, 5300 Patterson Avenue SE, Grand Rapids, MI 49530

Library of Congress Cataloging-in-Publication Data

Revolution devotional : 90 daily devotions for guys / Livingstone.
    p. cm.
  ISBN-13: 978-0-310-26706-5 (pbk.)
  1. Teenage boys--Religious life--Juvenile literature. 2. Devotional calendars--Juvenile
literature. I. Livingstone Corporation.

BV4541.3.R48 2005
242'.632--dc22

2005024202

Produced with the assistance of *Living*STONE (www.LivingstoneCorp.com).
Project staff includes Don Jones, Chris Hudson, and Randy Southern.

*Creative team: Dave Urbanski, Heather Haggerty, Anna Hammond,
and SharpSeven Design
Cover design by Holly Sharp
Printed in the United States of America*

>> Contents

>> First Things First

Dear Reader,

Are you wondering if this book is worth your time? It is, if any of the following apply to you:

You...

- Are looking for a daily devotional tool you can pick up and use *right now*.

- Want to develop the habit of spending time with God every day.

- Hope to see God grow your faith over the next 90 days.

- Want God to sharpen your character.

- Want to connect God's Word to the real issues in your life.

- Are looking for a cool companion product to *Revolution: The Bible for Teen Guys*.

- Like to read something challenging for your devotions.

Did any of those apply to you? If so, read on...

The *Revolution Devotional* contains 90 devotions written specifically for teenage guys. Here's the set-up: The devotions are arranged in 12 topical sections. Check out the Contents page to get a quick idea of what's inside.

Each day's devotion fills two pages. You'll read an opening verse, a devotion on a character trait or issue designed to challenge you to put what you read into practice *today*, a Bible passage, and a list of random entertaining/informative/ridiculous stuff.

Here's the deal: You can read the Bible 'til you pass out or lose your eyesight from staring at the little black text. You can read a devotional book every single day. But if it doesn't change how you live and who you are inside, then it's a waste of your time. So the challenge is not only to make this devotional book a part of your daily routine but also to boldly live out what God wants you to do. This is the greatest adventure of your life.

So quit reading the lousy introduction page and start living!

Randy Chris

SECTION 1

A Genuine Relationship with God

Going Deep with God

So in the course of time Hannah conceived and gave birth to a son. She named him Samuel, saying, "Because I asked the LORD for him."

1 Samuel 1:20

More than anything in the world, Hannah wanted a son. Unfortunately she wasn't able to get pregnant. So she did what any God-loving woman would do in her situation. She prayed about it. She took her troubles to God and begged him to help her.

Year after year after year.

Every chance she got, Hannah went to the house of the Lord to pray. As you might imagine, each year her prayers became a little more intense. She begged, pleaded, and cried for God to answer her. She vowed to dedicate her son to God if God would allow her to get pregnant. And in response, God finally gave her a son.

Hannah understood the value of constant prayer and worship. She never lost faith in God. She never stopped praising him. Maybe that's why God came through for her in such a big way.

Do you understand the value of prayer and worship in your life? Not just as a way to get the desires of your heart, but as a way to deepen your relationship with God?

Don't make the mistake of treating prayer like a drive-up window at a fast-food restaurant. Don't just place your order and then wait for God to fill it, expecting to get what you want and get it *now*. Instead work on developing a complete prayer and worship time with God.

And include more than just your requests in your private conversations with God. Praise him for who he is. Confess the things that have damaged your relationship with him. Thank him for the things he's done in your life. And when you're finished with those things, talk to him about your needs and desires.

It worked for Hannah. And it will work for you, too.

For the full story of how God rewarded Hannah's prayer of faith, check out 1 Samuel 1:1-28.

 ## Weird Things People Have Prayed For

The following list is real. People actually admitted to praying for these things. What odd prayers could you add to it?

- "During football season, I pray every Sunday that the Bears will win and the Packers will lose."

- "When I was little, I used to pray for cartoon characters like the Teenage Mutant Ninja Turtles and the X-Men."

- "I used to pray for lots of presents from Santa on Christmas."

- "This girl I liked was dating another guy, and I prayed she'd break up with him."

- "When I was late for curfew one night, I prayed that God would turn back time so I wouldn't get in trouble."

- "I used to pray that God would give me Kevin Garnet's basketball skills and give Garnet my skills."

- "After I bombed an English test, I prayed that God would burn the school down and destroy the evidence. I don't know why I didn't just pray for my test to get lost."

No Foolin'

Israel's arrogance testifies against him, but despite all this he does not return to the LORD his God or search for him.

Hosea 7:10

How real is your love for God? Do you believe in him when things are going bad just like you do when things are going great? Are you aware of him in your daily life, or is he just someone you think about for an hour or two on Sundays? Are you confident that you know him well, or is he really just an acquaintance to you?

One more question: If someone treated you the way you treat God, would you believe that person really loved you?

Faking a relationship with God isn't hard to do. You just need to know a little about the Bible...sprinkle a few Christian phrases in your conversations...maintain an upbeat attitude...and pretend to care about other people's problems. With a little effort, you could fool your parents, your youth leader, your girlfriend, and even your closest friends into believing that you're a faithful follower of Christ—when, in reality, you're nothing more than a spiritual poseur.

The two people you can't fool are you and God. If you don't have the fire of God's Holy Spirit in your heart, there's no way you can convince yourself that you do. And since God knows everything, he's not capable of being fooled.

That's why putting on a Christian act is ridiculous. Other people's opinions of your spiritual condition mean absolutely nothing in the long run. So you're left with a choice: either start a genuine relationship with God or abandon the whole Christian scene altogether.

Do yourself a favor: choose the first option. Stop trying to act like you think a Christian should act and start living according to God's Word. Stop trying to get credit for your spiritual resumé and start trying to please God with your life.

In other words...stop talking the talk and start walking the walk.

For more about how you can please God, check out Hosea 6:1-6.

 ## Blanking the Blank

"Walking the walk" and "talking the talk" are pretty common phrases—especially among Christians. But here are a few verb-noun combos that aren't nearly as well known. Can you believe that people actually say these?

1. Chalking the chalk

2. Stalking the stalk

3. Boring the bore

4. Ducking the duck

5. Winding the wind

6. Jamming the jam

7. Hiding the hide

8. Creeping the creep

9. Freaking the freak

10. Teaching the teach

Stirred, Not Shaken

The men of Israel were subdued on that occasion, and the men of Judah were victorious because they relied on the LORD, the God of their fathers.

2 Chronicles 13:18

Abijah's army of Judah was outnumbered 800,000 to 400,000. His Israelite opponents had enough men to attack full-strength from the front and the rear. Those aren't the kind of scouting reports you want to hear when you're facing a life-and-death situation. To most observers, the outlook for Judah seemed bleak.

Yet when the time for battle came, Abijah never even hesitated. He and his men ignored the odds stacked against them. They engaged in battle with the spirit of champions, not underdogs. It's not that they were overly impressed with their own fighting skills. No, Abijah and his men were confident because they relied on God. Abijah did what he believed was right and trusted God to help him deal with the outcome. (You'll find the results of the battle in the verse above.)

Do you have that kind of confident faith in God?

Chances are you've faced your share of situations in which you felt outnumbered or overpowered—whether at home, at school, or at work. Perhaps it's a parent who refuses to talk about spiritual things. Or a teacher who seems to take delight in shooting down your beliefs. Or a boss who schedules you to work every Sunday morning, even after you've ask him not to.

If your confidence has been shaken by a particular situation, it's time to renew your strength. Invite God into the battle. Put your trust in him. Let him reverse the odds for you. And then do what Abijah and his men did. Tackle the situation with the spirit of a champion. Refuse to think of yourself as an underdog. Remind yourself who has your back. Rely on him to guide you...protect you...bless your efforts...and engineer an eventual victory.

To find out the nitty gritty about Abijah's remarkable faith in God, read 2 Chronicles 13:1-14:1.

 **Reliance Testers**

It's a good idea to rely on God. And some situations call for a little *extra* reliance. Such as...

1. When your girlfriend says, "We need to talk."

2. When the pilot says, "Ladies and gentlemen, we will be experiencing severe turbulence for the next hour or so."

3. When your teacher says, "We need to talk."

4. When you see red lights flashing in your rear-view mirror.

5. When your parents say, "We need to talk."

6. When you go to the free-throw line for two shots...with no time left on the clock...and your team is trailing by one.

SECTION 1: A GENUINE RELATIONSHIP WITH GOD

No Matter What

Though the fig tree does not bud and there are no grapes on the vines, though the olive crop fails and the fields produce no food, though there are no sheep in the pen and no cattle in the stalls, yet I will rejoice in the LORD, I will be joyful in God my Savior.

Habakkuk 3:17-18

When was the last time you fired off a prayer like Habakkuk's in the passage above? Habakkuk wanted God to know that his faithfulness and joy didn't depend on his circumstances. No matter what happened, Habakkuk was committed to his Savior. If you're looking for a short-term goal in your Christian walk, try preparing yourself to offer a similar prayer of unconditional faithfulness to God.

Think about times when you've had trouble recognizing God's blessings in your life. Times when two or three difficult situations popped up at once and caused you to lose sight of the good things God has done for you. Ask God to forgive you for your shortsightedness. Make a commitment not to lose sight of his work again. Ask him to keep your vision clear so that you can see the good as well as the bad in your life. And then say a big "thank you" for all the things he does.

You might also want to memorize a few Bible passages that you can cling to in tough times to help you fulfill your commitment. You could start with the passage above. After you've mastered that one, you could move on to, say, Psalm 23:4 ("Even though I walk through the valley of the shadow of death, I will fear no evil, for you are with me; your rod and your staff, they comfort me"). Keep God's Word close to your heart. That way, when tough times come—and they will come—you'll have your response ready. You'll have a head start on remaining faithful to God. Not to mention the security, comfort, and protection that comes from staying close to him.

It takes a strong person to be able to say with Habakkuk, "Yet I will rejoice in the Lord." Are you that person?

For Habakkuk's entire prayer, see Habakkuk 3:1-19.

Weird Things to Be Thankful For

Habakkuk was thankful when he had no crops and cattle. We present the following list of items for which you have probably never thought to be thankful. Aren't you glad that...

- deodorant was invented.

- the homecoming queen wasn't following you during your first time behind the wheel.

- it's no longer cool for guys to wear short shorts.

- braces aren't permanent.

- the picture on your license isn't the picture used in the yearbook.

- you'll never have to repeat that first day of freshman orientation.

- when you take your shirt off for swim class, you can focus on the fact that you haven't stopped growing yet.

Been There, Done That

For we do not have a high priest who is unable to sympathize with our weaknesses, but we have one who has been tempted in every way, just as we are—yet was without sin.

Hebrews 4:15

There are two kinds of role models: the ones who say, "Do as I say and not as I do," and the ones who say, "Follow my example." Chances are you've known some people who fit into the first category—men and women whose positions demanded respect but whose actions have made them less than respect-worthy. Maybe it was a teacher who tried too hard to be one of the guys. Or a scout leader whose private life turned out to be...messy, to say the least. How hard is it to take advice from people like that? To get life lessons from those who obviously haven't put those lessons to practice in their own lives?

The author of the book of Hebrews makes it clear that Jesus definitely belongs in the second category of "follow my example" role models and leaders. Not only did he talk the talk, he walked the walk. In other words, he doesn't ask us to do anything he didn't do himself. Jesus had to deal with the same emotions you struggle with. He faced the same major temptations you face. (In fact, he went toe-to-toe with Satan, the great tempter.) The difference is, Jesus never gave in to temptation. He never allowed his urges to get the better of him. He left the earth with the only perfect record against sin.

That's great news for you. You see, no matter what you're going through, Jesus can relate to it. He can direct you—drawing not just on his unlimited wisdom but also on his personal experience. Even better, he can give you the strength you need to be victorious over sin.

All you have to do is call on him. The next time temptation comes calling, or the next time life seems confusing, contact Jesus, the world's greatest high priest.

If you're interested in Jesus' credentials as a high priest, check out Hebrews 4:14-5:10.

 ## Recognizing Bad Leaders

We mentioned earlier that there are good leaders and not-so-good leaders. But how do you tell the difference? Here are some obvious clues for spotting a bad leader:

1. He has his own police mug shot framed on his desk.

2. He tells you to do something. You do it and get into all kinds of trouble. He says, "That's the exact same thing that happened to me."

3. He is unable to say, "You must respect me," with a straight face.

4. He constantly asks you what he can do to look cooler.

5. When someone asks him what makes him a good leader, he mentions his extreme hunger for power.

It's about Time

I call on you, O God, for you will answer me;
give ear to me and hear my prayer.

Psalm 17:6

Think of the most desperate prayer you've ever prayed. Maybe it was for a terminally ill loved one. Or for your parents to stop fighting. Or for a girlfriend to take you back. Or for a personal problem that seemed unsolvable. Or for a situation that seemed hopeless.

How did God respond to your prayer? Did he answer right away, exactly as you were hoping? Did he take some time to resolve the situation, perhaps in a way you weren't expecting? Did he help you see the situation from a different perspective, one that changed the way you prayed about it? Or are you still waiting for an answer from him?

Whatever the case, chances are you've asked yourself the same question Christians have asked for centuries: *Why does God take his time answering prayers?*

For one thing, God can see things we can't. All of time—past, present, and future—is laid out before him. He can see what lies ahead. What's more, he can see the consequences of every action. He knows exactly what will happen if a prayer is answered tomorrow...or next month...or three years from now.

Remember, God wants what's best for you *in the long run.* He won't sacrifice his long-term plan to give you temporary relief or pleasure. Because of his perfect knowledge, God knows exactly what to do and when to do it, so he's never actually late in answering any prayer. But since you don't know when his answer will come or what his answer will be, your best bet is to keep praying and get on with living your faith journey.

Don't get upset with God for answers to prayer that seem overdue to you. Instead, ask him for the patience to wait for his will and the wisdom to recognize it when it comes.

To read about what Jesus said about prayer, check out Luke 11:1-13.

 ## Seven Things You Can Do While You Wait for God

1. Come up with a rhyme for the word *orange*.

2. Answer this question: Why do people park in a driveway and drive on a parkway?

3. Think of another word for *synonym*.

4. Come up with a twenty-seventh letter of the alphabet—something to go between "K" and "L."

5. Figure out why a baseball player can hit a ball traveling 100 miles per hour in front of 50,000 screaming fans, but a golfer needs complete silence to hit a stationary ball.

6. Write a song in pig Latin.

7. Discover where chalk goes when it's erased.

Time to Grow Up

Anyone who lives on milk, being still an infant, is not acquainted with the teaching about righteousness. But solid food is for the mature, who by constant use have trained themselves to distinguish good from evil.

Hebrews 5:13-14

What happened after you learned the basics of addition and subtraction? You kept moving up, right? First you go to algebra, then geometry, then trig and calculus, and all those other GPA-killing classes. How frustrating would it be for a graduating senior still to be reviewing his multiplication tables when he should be studying calculus?

The same thing goes for your faith. It's not enough to just keep reviewing the "basics" of salvation over and over again. Or to keep rehashing the same well-known Bible stories you've heard since you were little. There's no growth in that.

The author of the book of Hebrews makes it clear that believers have a responsibility to move to higher levels of Christian maturity. That means digging deeper into God's Word. Exploring books you've never read before—even those in the Old Testament. Learning to tell the difference between God's truth and false teachings. Finding ways to apply the principles of Scripture to your everyday life.

If you neglect your responsibility, you will remain a spiritual infant. A milk drinker. An immature believer. And a squanderer of potential.

Notice the words we used in the previous paragraph: *your responsibility.* You are the one who must take charge of your Christian maturing process. You can't pass off the responsibility to your parents...

or your Sunday school teacher...or your youth leader...or your pastor. None of those people will have to answer to God for your spiritual growth. But you will.

That doesn't mean you're on your own, though. Far from it. If you're serious about becoming a more mature believer, God will bring people into your life to assist you. He'll also bless your efforts to understand his Word by giving you the wisdom and insight you need.

For more about the dangers of spiritual immaturity, check out Hebrews 5:11-6:12.

 ## Signs That You Need to Do Some Spiritual Maturing

- You'd rather clean drool off the toys in the nursery than sit through a sermon on Sunday morning.

- Your Bible study journal contains more doodles and tic-tac-toe games than journaling.

- The pages of the Old Testament in your Bible have fused together as a result of non-use.

- You're still surprised by the ending of the Easter story.

- Wearing a T-shirt of your favorite Christian band is the closest you've ever come to sharing your faith.

Dig In

*Do your best to present yourself to God as one approved,
a workman who does not need to be ashamed
and who correctly handles the word of truth.*

2 Timothy 2:15

Do you have an inquisitive nature? Are you constantly looking to expand your knowledge? Do you get a rush when you discover something new? If so, does your curiosity and hunger for knowledge carry over to your Bible study? It should.

God doesn't lay out everything we need to know on the first page of Genesis. His goal isn't to make our Christian walk as easy as possible. He wants to see commitment on our part. He wants us to be willing to dig for what he has to offer. So when you open God's Word, you must be prepared to work. That means when you come across a Scripture passage you have a hard time understanding, you can't just shrug your shoulders and skip it. Instead you need to commit yourself to figuring out what the passage means and why God put it in the Bible.

If that means pulling a Bible commentary from your grandpa's bookshelf or researching the passage in a study Bible, do it. If it means checking out a Bible Q&A page on the Web or talking to your youth leader or church pastor about it, do it. The Bible isn't always easy to understand, but it's always well worth the effort to understand.

The more you dig into Scripture, the more connections you'll find. Almost like a jigsaw puzzle. As you turn over pieces and begin to fit them together, you'll start to see the big picture. Things that seemed totally random and confusing before will start to make sense.

To learn more about the awesome power of Bible study, read 2 Timothy 3:14-16.

 Nagging Questions from the Bible

1. Why did Adam come up with cool names for some animals—like the jaguar and rhinoceros—and dull, obvious names for other animals—like the bear and anteater?

2. Who did Cain, Adam and Eve's first son, marry?

3. How could Noah tell the difference between a male and female salamander?

4. How long do you think it took Mephibosheth's friends to come up with a shorter nickname for him?

5. If the prophet Amos' last name had been "Quito," would it have affected the way people responded to him?

6. Why would any parent name a daughter Gomer? (See Hosea 1:3.)

7. Read Luke 22:38. We know Peter was armed with one sword on the night Jesus was arrested (see John 18:10). Who else was packing steel that night?

8. Since 2 John is so short, shouldn't it be called a memo instead of a letter?

Give Up?

*"Cursed is the cheat who has an acceptable male in his flock and vows to give it, but then sacrifices a blemished animal to the Lord. For I am a great king," says the L*ORD* Almighty, "and my name is to be feared among the nations."*

Malachi 1:14

Before Jesus' once-and-for-all sacrifice on the cross, God's people had to offer several different sacrifices every year in order to maintain their relationship with him. There were sin offerings, thanksgiving offerings, freewill offerings, festival offerings—just to mention a few. Each offering had its own special requirements. Most of them involved killing livestock.

But the one common denominator of all Old Testament offerings is that God expected the absolute best from his people. If the offering called for a young bull, God expected the person offering the sacrifice to use the best young bull in his herd. If the sacrifice called for a lamb, God expected the sacrifice of a spotless lamb—one without any blemishes.

Fortunately for us, God no longer requires us to offer him livestock. But that doesn't mean he still doesn't desire—and reward—sacrifice. And that's a golden opportunity for you—if you're prepared to take advantage of it.

What kind of sacrifice does God want from us today? Simply put, he wants *us*. He wants us to give him our heart, mind, and will. And we do this by loving and worshipping him and by obeying his commands and putting him first in our lives (Romans 12:1).

Offering ourselves to God is primarily a matter of the heart, but it shows up in how we live our lives, too. You can offer yourself to God in very practical ways. What can you give to God as a sacrifice to demonstrate how important he is to you? How about your time? Would you be willing to carve out a two- or three-hour block of your weekend and devote that time to one of your church's service ministries?

How about your money? Would you be willing to give up entertainment (including fast food, movies, and video games) each month and use the money you save to help sponsor a child in another country who needs food, medicine, and education?

Keep in mind that God wants prime sacrifices, not leftovers. If you are putting God first in your life, you'll give him the best of what you have. He wants your whole being, not just what you have to spare.

For more of God's instructions concerning sacrifices, check out Malachi 1:6-14.

 Don't-Bother Sacrifices

Some sacrificial acts leave much to be desired. Here are a few that probably don't qualify as offerings:

- Giving up tofu and radishes for God's sake.

- Splitting your discount oil-change coupons with God.

- In lieu of the Old Testament requirement of a real bull, pouring out the contents of a Red Bull energy drink on your front lawn.

- Parting with a Christmas fruitcake in honor of Jesus' birth.

- Setting fire to "unblemished" logs in your fireplace when it's cold outside.

Hold Tight

Rescue me from my enemies, O LORD, for I hide myself in you.

Psalm 143:9

As the king of Israel, David had a lot of problems with enemies. Those outside—and inside—his kingdom were always opposing him. Each time his enemies attacked, David's first response was to talk to God about it. The king made a habit of taking his problems to God...again and again and again.

In this entry's opening verse, for what seems like the thousandth time in the book of Psalms, David begs God to rescue him from his enemies. You'd think that after a while God would say, "Enough already! Stop asking me to rescue you!" But he doesn't do that to David. And he won't do that to you. You see, God is infinitely more patient than we are. He doesn't get annoyed by repetitive prayer requests. He *wants* you to bring your problems and fears to him...as often as you need to.

Do you have any ongoing prayer requests? Needs or concerns that you've taken to God time after time? Do you wonder whether God will ever answer you? If so, take a cue from David.

If you believe your prayer request is something that aligns with God's will, keep praying. Be persistent. Don't let your confidence waver. And don't let the fact that you haven't gotten an answer yet discourage you. Remember, God has his own schedule for doing things. Commit yourself to waiting on him. But don't be shy about repeating your request—in a respectful way, of course.

If you're not sure whether your prayer request aligns with God's will, ask God for the wisdom and insight to decide. You might also want to get input from mature Christians whose opinions you trust—perhaps your parents, your pastor, or your youth leader.

If you get a clear signal that your request is out of bounds, cut it from your prayers. If not, keep praying. Give God a chance to reward your persistence.

For the full impact of David's persistent prayer, take a look at Psalm 143:1-12.

 ## Bad Ideas When You're Waiting for God

- Putting him on a stopwatch to see how long it takes him to respond to your prayer requests.

- Threatening to take your business elsewhere if he doesn't give you what you want.

- Rolling your eyes, sighing heavily, and tapping your foot impatiently.

- Demanding to talk to his manager.

- Filling out a complaint card against him and dropping it in the offering plate at church.

- Boycotting prayer.

World-Class Prayers

I am like a desert owl, like an owl among the ruins. I lie awake;
I have become like a bird alone on a roof.

Psalm 102:6-7

On a scale of one to 10, how would you rate yourself as a pray-er? Don't just think in terms of how often you pray or how long you pray; think about the prayers themselves. How much thought do you put into your words to God?

Many Christians treat prayer like instant messages to friends. They communicate the necessary information as quickly and efficiently as possible and then sign off—hoping for an equally quick and efficient response, of course. And in the process they lose sight of what prayer can and should be. The best way to see what prayer can be is to check out the book of Psalms. Say what you want about poetry and the people who write it; the fact remains that the psalmists were world-class pray-ers. They knew how to send up words that pleased God.

One thing that made the psalmists such great pray-ers is that they worked hard to keep their prayers fresh, interesting, and heartfelt. They used their God-given creativity to express their true feelings in original and innovative ways. In the verses above, the psalmist could have said, "God, I feel lonely." Instead he uses what he knows about nature to get his point across in a more poetic way. (In case you're wondering, desert owls live in isolated, lonely places.)

Does God demand that kind of creativity in every prayer? Of course not. Does he appreciate the effort? What do you think?

What steps can you take to punch up your prayer life? You don't have to come up with poetry, if that's not your thing. But you should do what you can to keep your prayer life exciting, fun, and out of the ordinary.

To get the big picture of the psalmist's creativity, read Psalm 102:1-28.

 Creative Prayer Ideas That May Not Work

- Echoing a friend's prayer one word at a time.

- Beginning each prayer with a knock-knock joke.

- Trying a different accent every time you pray.

- Praying backwards—starting your prayer with "Amen" and ending with "Father Heavenly Dear."

- One-word prayers.

- Late-night prayer marathons, sprawled on your bed with a pillow under your head.

- Trying to say an entire prayer without using a word that starts with a vowel.

What's on Your Mind?

Do not let this Book of the Law depart from your mouth; meditate on it day and night, so that you may be careful to do everything written in it. Then you will be prosperous and successful.

Joshua 1:8

The Bible is a rather large book and can be overwhelming to read sometimes. But as a Christian, the Bible is your lifeline. It's God's Word to you. You need to read it. There's only one way to get comfortable with the Bible, and that's to spend a lot of time in it. You'll find that once you get comfortable, a whole new world of spiritual understanding opens up to you.

Reading the Bible is a great way to discover who God is and his will for your life. And memorizing Scripture verses is a great way to make sure that God's principles are never far from your mind.

That's important when you're facing scary or uncertain circumstances in your life. You'll find that God's Holy Spirit often helps you recall just the right words of comfort at just the right time. And while those words may not change your circumstances, they will give you the strength you need to face them. The same goes for times when you're hit with a real temptation to sin. If you load your mind with passages of God's Word, you'll discover the Holy Spirit uses them as ammunition to help you fight your way out of sticky and tempting situations.

But don't take our word for it. See for yourself. You'll find that meditating on God's Word—thinking about it constantly, praying for God to help you understand it more clearly, searching for ways to use its truth in your everyday life—is a great way to change your heart forever.

REVOLUTION DEVOTIONAL

For more of God's instructions to Joshua, check out Joshua 1:1-18.

 Five Radical Ideas for Keeping Scripture Close 24-7

Does God's command to meditate on his Word day and night seem impossible to you? Here are five suggestions that may (or may not) help:

1. Wear gospel pajamas (with glow-in-the-dark Bible verses on them) to bed every night.

2. Load up your iPod with about 200 hours of Bible reading.

3. Hang a billboard outside your bedroom window that displays a new Scripture passage every week.

4. Hire someone to instant message Bible verses to you every 20 minutes.

5. Ask your cable provider to start carrying the Bible Verse Network.

Thanksgiving Every Day

If he offers it as an expression of thankfulness, then along with this thank offering he is to offer cakes of bread made without yeast and mixed with oil, wafers made without yeast and spread with oil, and cakes of fine flour well-kneaded and mixed with oil.

Leviticus 7:12

Would you say it's easier to be a follower of God today than it was back in ancient Israel? Look again at the verse for this entry. When the Israelites gave a thanksgiving offering, they had to mix special dough with oil, knead it, and make little cakes of bread without yeast. And that was just one of many kinds of offerings they had to give in their worship.

Compared to them, we've got it made. When we want to offer thanks to God, all we have to do is stop, bow our heads, and say a quick prayer. What could be easier?

Unfortunately, no matter how convenient it is for us to show thankfulness to God, there will always be distractions and obstacles to keep us from doing it. We live in a busy world. There are lots of different things vying for our attention. School. Sports. Girls. Homework. Video games. TV. Friends. With so much going on, we lose track of the things God does for us. And we let them go unmentioned—even though our mothers taught us to say "thank you" when someone does something nice for us.

How do you feel when you do something nice for someone, only to have that person ignore your niceness? How do you think God feels when we do the same thing to him? Are you guilty of taking God for granted?

What is your blessing-to-thanking ratio? To figure it out, compare the number of things God does for you every day to the number of things you *specifically* thank him for on a daily basis. Obviously we're not talking exact figures here, but you should be able to come up with a ballpark estimate. What do you think your ratio is—100 to one? 1,000 to one?

If you want to improve your relationship with God, make an effort to lower that ratio by simply noticing and thanking him for the many things he does for you every day.

To jog your memory about some other things to thank God for, read through Psalm 103.

 ## More Weird Things to Be Thankful For

Aren't you thankful that...

- you don't squirt a nasty-smelling scent when people startle you, as skunks do?

- sand isn't part of your recommended daily diet?

- your most embarrassing dreams aren't broadcast on satellite TV?

- video game characters can't take revenge on you for the things you do to them?

- the legal driving age isn't 55?

- the top of your head isn't transparent, with your brain visible for everyone to see?

- you don't get grades in Sunday school?

SECTION 2

God's Identity

Let's Get Serious

The LORD has given full vent to his wrath; he has poured out his fierce anger. He kindled a fire in Zion that consumed her foundations.

Lamentations 4:11

Nothing is scarier than being on the receiving end of God's wrath. When God pours out his anger, no one and nothing is safe. Just ask the Israelites.

The people of Israel lost everything they had. Their homes were destroyed. They were kidnapped. They were forced to move to a foreign country. They were held as prisoners. What brought on such disaster? The Israelites disobeyed God. It's that simple. They refused to live by his laws, and he allowed them to suffer the consequences.

That's how seriously God treats sin.

Too bad more people don't share his attitude. Many believers approach sin believing that since Jesus already paid the price for our sins, we can do pretty much whatever we want without worrying about punishment. They treat God's forgiveness like a credit card ("I'll just put this sin on Jesus' tab"). They figure if Jesus died for all the sins of the world, a few more here and there won't make any difference.

But that attitude completely misses the point of Jesus' sacrifice. Jesus didn't die to make it easier for us to sin. He died to break sin's power over us. Thanks to Jesus, we're no longer slaves to our sinful impulses. With his help, we have the power to overcome them.

If that's not motivation enough to rethink your attitude toward sin, try this: God's attitude toward sin hasn't changed since his son's sacrifice. He still will not tolerate disobedience. And just because you haven't been carried off to a foreign land doesn't mean you won't suffer the consequences of your sinful choices.

For one thing, your sins separate you from God. You can't have a tight relationship with him if you're off chasing every whim that seems exciting to you. You'll feel distant from him. And the only way to bridge that gap and make things right is to turn away from sin.

For more of God's brutally honest assessment of his people, check out Lamentations 4:1-22.

 Signs That Show You Might Not Be Taking Sin Seriously Enough

- Someone yells, "Hey, sinner!" and you assume he's talking to you.

- You need more than two solid days to confess your sins in prayer.

- You have a bumper sticker that reads, "I can resist anything but temptation."

- You consider Lamentations the funniest book of the Bible.

- While working on a crossword puzzle, your mom asks for a synonym for *wickedness,* and your dad suggests your name.

- Drug dealers refuse to hang out with you because they say you're a bad influence.

- Your favorite hymn is "Anything Goes."

Skeleton Crew

The hand of the L<small>ORD</small> was upon me, and he brought me out by the Spirit of the L<small>ORD</small> and set me in the middle of a valley; it was full of bones...So I prophesied as I was commanded. And as I was prophesying, there was a noise, a rattling sound, and the bones came together, bone to bone. I looked, and tendons and flesh appeared on them and skin covered them, but there was no breath in them.

Ezekiel 37:1, 7-8

Skeletons coming to life? Sounds like something from a horror movie—not something you'd read about in the Bible. But this was no mere spook house designed to give Ezekiel a few thrills and chills. This happens to be one of the coolest demonstrations of God's power in all of the Old Testament.

Think about it. The bones in the valley were dry, which means the blood and other body fluids that gave them life had long since drained from them. The flesh that surrounded the bones had been picked clean by birds of prey. So there was nothing left but the skeletal reminders of what had once been. Medically speaking, the situation was hopeless. The bones were dead—with no chance of their condition changing.

Until God stepped in.

God wanted to help Ezekiel understand that nothing is hopeless where he is concerned. And what better way to do it than giving old bones new life?

Are you facing any hopeless situations in your life? Maybe your parents have given up on their marriage. Maybe you or someone you love is facing a serious health crisis. Maybe you're struggling with academics and wondering how you'll ever make it to college. Don't despair.

Regardless of how bleak your situation seems, you have to admit that it's not quite as hopeless as a valley full of dry bones. And look what God did with that!

While you're on this planet, you're never too broken for God to fix. No matter what you're facing, you have hope. Nothing is beyond his ability to repair and restore. As Ezekiel discovered, God's awesome power can accomplish things beyond anyone's imagination.

Are you ready to give him a chance?

To get the full story of Ezekiel's skeleton crew, see Ezekiel 37:1-14.

Optional Miracles

Reattaching flesh to bones was certainly an impressive feat. But there are other ways God could have made his point to Ezekiel. For example, he might have...

- moved the waters of the Red Sea to where Ezekiel was standing—and then parted them so Ezekiel could walk through.

- turned Ezekiel into a skeleton—a walking, talking skeleton.

- given the skeletons musical instruments and turned them into a band, instead of an army.

- shown Ezekiel some freaky visions...oh, right, he already did that in Ezekiel 1.

- had Ezekiel fight and defeat the army of skeletons—with nothing but a leg bone.

The Conquering King

Out of his mouth comes a sharp sword with which to strike down the nations. "He will rule them with an iron scepter." He treads the winepresses of the fury of the wrath of God Almighty. On his robe and on his thigh he has this name written: KING OF KINGS AND LORD OF LORDS.

Revelation 19:15-16

Jesus came once to earth, died, rose again, and then he returned to his Father. The Bible also teaches that Jesus will come again for his own. And the book of Revelation gives us a glimpse of the events that will surround Jesus' return to earth. While the complex imagery that John, the author, uses in Revelation makes it tough to say exactly what will happen, three truths come through quite clearly. One: Jesus' return will be awesome for his people. Two: Jesus' return will be terrifying for his enemies. Three: Jesus' return will be nothing like his first arrival.

The first time Jesus came to our planet, it was as a tiny, helpless baby. The next time, it will be as the conquering Warrior and King. Nothing will stand in his way. His enemies will be defeated. His followers will be rewarded. His judgment will be carried out. When Jesus returns, everyone who rejected him or wrote him off as nothing more than a teacher or philosopher will see him as he really is—in all of his glory and power. Only then will they understand the consequences of rejecting Christ. The *eternal* consequences of rejecting him.

Take some time to think about the awesome reality of Jesus' return. Ask God to let the truth of it sink in. Really sink in. If this truth gets hold of you, you will begin to change. Distractions such as popularity, porn, or whatever other garbage you're tempted with will begin to look pretty dull in comparison to the mind-blowing glory of what's coming. Resolve to become consumed with the return of Christ, and you'll have a serious weapon against the temptations of the world.

For more information about the awe-inspiring return of the King, check out Revelation 19:11-21 and Matthew 24:30-31.

 ## What *Not* to be Consumed With

God wants us to become consumed with the return of Christ. Here are a few things *not* to become consumed with:

- Looking like a rock star or movie star.

- Sumo wrestling.

- Playing the most humiliating practical joke possible on your history teacher.

- Beating your favorite video game.

- Wearing the color pink.

- Antagonizing your sibling to the point of a mental breakdown.

- Breaking the "highest vocal note ever sung by a male" world record.

It's All Lies!

Have nothing to do with godless myths and old wives' tales; rather, train yourself to be godly.

1 Timothy 4:7

Timothy wasn't the only one who had to worry about "godless myths" and "old wives' tales." Here are a few popular ideas you need to recognize as lies today:

Lie #1: It doesn't matter what you believe about spiritual things, as long as you believe in something. Wrong. All the belief in the world can't make something true. Jesus said he alone is the way to eternal life with God. He is the only one worthy of our belief.

Lie #2: Jesus had some good ideas, but he wasn't the Son of God. If Jesus wasn't the Son of God, he's a liar. And that means everything he ever said should be rejected. But Jesus proved his divine nature by the miracles he performed, the sinless life he lived, the changes he made in people's lives, and the victory he claimed over death.

Lie #3: It's only a sin if it hurts someone else. We don't get to decide what is and isn't sin. God does. And his standard is much higher than ours. Anything that violates his Word is a sin.

Lie #4: If you contribute to a certain ministry, God will make you wealthy. Nowhere in the Bible does God promise material wealth as a reward for serving him. Tithing is a way to faithfully give back to God some of what he's given to us. It's not a get-rich-quick scheme.

Lie #5: If you can't accept someone's lifestyle, you're being narrow-minded. If narrow-minded means allowing God's Word to influence your opinion of right and wrong, then there's nothing wrong with being narrow-minded. God doesn't give us the right to pronounce judgment on other people, but he does encourage us to stand up for what's right and speak out against what's wrong.

Godliness and lies can't coexist. If you're serious about living for Christ, you need to identify these and other misconceptions for the lies they are.

See what other advice Paul gave to Timothy in 1 Timothy 4:1-16.

 ## Knowing What *Not* to Believe

Speaking of myths and lies, here are some more to add to the list:

1. Cramming for 10 minutes just before a test should get you a passing grade.

2. All you need to do is find the right body spray, and girls will throw themselves at you.

3. Most cops don't even consider it speeding unless you're doing at least 20 m.p.h. over the speed limit.

4. Playing "How Crazy Are You?" with matches and gasoline is fun.

5. Driving with your knees is okay if you're trying to eat a cheeseburger in the car.

A Mighty Friend

When I consider your heavens, the work of your fingers, the moon and the stars, which you have set in place, what is man that you are mindful of him, the son of man that you care for him?

Psalm 8:3-4

Imagine you get home from school one day to find the president of the United States sitting in your living room. "I was concerned about you today," he explains. "So I thought I'd stop by to talk for a while."

Once you get over your shock, you sit down and have a nice, long conversation with him. To your amazement, he knows the details of your life. What's more, he listens intently as you share your thoughts and feelings. When you're done, he hands you a card with his private phone number on it. Then the leader of the free world says to you, "If you need anything, give me a call. I have the power to help you, no matter what your problem is."

Unbelievable, right? After all, who's ever been given an opportunity like that?

Actually, each one of us is given that opportunity every day. Not with the president, but with one who's infinitely more important and powerful.

Think about this: The God who carved out the Grand Canyon cares about the things going on in your family. The God who raised up Mount Everest is concerned about how you're dealing with pressure at school. The God who filled the Pacific Ocean has a personal interest in the way you spend your weekends. The God who put every star and planet in the universe in its place wants to hear from you and talk to you every day.

How should you respond to that kind of attention? The same way David did—with complete awe and wonder.

Take a few minutes today to express your gratitude to God in a meaningful way. You can follow David's lead and write a psalm of amazement. Or better yet, you can use your God-given talents to express yourself in a drawing...a poem...a song...a piano or guitar solo...or anything else that pops into your head.

For more of David's words of amazement and gratitude, read Psalm 8:1-9.

 ## You've Got It Made

Having the Almighty God—the all-knowing, all-powerful, loving Creator of the universe—take a personal interest in you is kind of like...

- Steven Spielberg shooting your family videos;

- The *Extreme Makeover* team helping you get ready for a date;

- Martha Stewart cleaning your room;

- Dale Earnhardt, Jr. driving you to school;

- The United States Army's 1st Infantry backing you up when you confront a bully;

- Bill Gates sponsoring your Young Entrepreneurs Club;

- LeBron James pairing up with you in a two-on-two basketball tournament;

- Stephen King helping you with a creative writing assignment; *...only much, much better!*

SECTION 3

Being a Man of Faith

More Than Just Talk

But someone will say, "You have faith; I have deeds." Show me your faith without deeds, and I will show you my faith by what I do.

James 2:18

Put up or shut up. That's the basic message James is trying to communicate in this verse. If all you're going to do is *talk* about how much God means to you...how drastically he's changed your life...and how strong your commitment to him is, you're better off keeping your mouth shut.

Think about it in movie terms. Which would you rather watch: a film depicting people sitting around and talking about their lives or a blowout, action blockbuster? If you're like most guys, you want action. So do the people who are curious about the Christian faith. Which means you must be prepared to walk the walk if you're going to talk the talk.

Putting your faith in Jesus means believing that his plan for your life is the best possible one. And if you *really* believe his plan is best, then you'll commit to following his instructions about how to live. You'll change your actions to accommodate your faith. Otherwise it's just a bunch of talk.

If you follow God's instructions, you will help people in need, forgive those who hurt you, and tell people about Jesus, among other things. If you're not currently doing these things, you need to take a closer look at your faith. Something may be missing. And if that's the case, you won't be the only one who suffers. Whether you realize it or not, people are watching *you*. Unbelievers who know about your Christian faith will look to you to see what Christianity is all about.

And if they see that you're not putting your money where your mouth is, they may decide that Christianity is a crock.

You see, if there's one thing people won't tolerate, it's a hypocrite. Especially one who claims to follow Christ.

If you are curious about the relationship between faith and deeds, check out James 2:14-26.

 Faith Without Deeds?

Claiming to have faith in Christ without demonstrating it in the way you live is like...

- telling friends about the best restaurant you've ever frequented, dropping them off at the door—and then going to a fast-food joint down the street for your meal.

- a magician describing to an audience the details of his most incredible magic trick—and then walking off the stage.

- a guy giving an engagement ring to his girlfriend as a sign of lifelong commitment, devotion, and faithfulness—and then playing the field.

- a football player talking trash about an opponent the night before a game—and then refusing to play the next day.

Unleashing Your Inner Warrior

Do not suppose that I have come to bring peace to the earth.
I did not come to bring peace, but a sword.

Matthew 10:34

The words in the verse above come from Jesus himself. Does it surprise you that the Prince of Peace would say something like that? It shouldn't.

You see, Jesus' teachings are extremely unpopular with most human beings. Sacrificing pleasure for obedience? Putting other people's needs ahead of your own? Showing love to enemies? Those aren't the kind of teachings people want to hear. And they *really* don't want to hear that they're sinners who need to be forgiven in order to have eternal life.

So those of us who identify ourselves as Jesus' disciples should expect opposition—that's the "sword" part Jesus was talking about. Those of us who choose to spread his message to others should expect occasional hostility.

If you're serious about living a life that's pleasing to God, there's no escaping the consequences. Even among the people closest to you. Unless everyone you care about is a Christian, at some point your faith is going to cause some friction between you and a friend or family member. Then you'll be faced with a choice. You can either sweep your faith under the rug and agree not to talk about it in order to keep the peace, or you can make it clear to the person how much your faith means to you and let God worry about protecting the relationship.

Your choice will say a lot about your priorities. About whether your relationships with your friends and family mean more to you than your relationship with God.

Jesus makes it clear that conflict isn't necessarily a bad thing. That doesn't mean you should go around looking for theological fights. But it also means you shouldn't back down when people disagree with you. You may find that some people are motivated by the strength of your convictions. When they see how strong your faith is, they may be inspired to investigate Jesus for themselves.

To see how you can endure opposition, read Hebrews 12:1-3.

 Less-Than-Ideal Ways to Handle Opposition to Your Faith

1. Challenging an opponent to a duel.

2. Arguing that Jesus is better looking than any other spiritual leader—including Buddha and Mohammed.

3. Responding with "I'm rubber and you're glue—everything you say bounces off me and sticks to you."

4. Giving up your faith and joining the opposition.

5. Chanting, "Go home, heathen, go home!"

6. Laughing at misguided notions concerning the Bible.

7. Repeatedly slapping your opponent.

Hardcore

If we are thrown into the blazing furnace, the God we serve is able to save us from it, and he will rescue us from your hand, O king. But even if he does not, we want you to know, O king, that we will not serve your gods or worship the image of gold you have set up.

Daniel 3:17-18

Here's the situation: King Nebuchadnezzar commissioned the creation of a giant statue of himself and summoned all of the officials in his kingdom to its dedication. The rules of the dedication were simple: When the music started, everyone had to bow down and worship the statue. Anyone who refused would get tossed into a blazing furnace. For most of the weasels who served under Nebuchadnezzar, that was no problem. They would have bowed down to a head of lettuce if ol' Neb had told them to.

But for three transplanted Israelites, Nebuchadnezzar's order posed a huge problem. Shadrach, Meshach, and Abednego worshipped God. Period. There was no way they could bow down to an idol. They had no choice but to disobey Nebuchadnezzar's order.

On Dedication Day, when the music started, Shadrach, Meshach, and Abednego stood while everyone else bowed. And when Nebuchadnezzar heard about it, he was royally ticked. He had the three men brought before him and gave them one more chance. He warned them they would be incinerated if they refused—and that no god would be able to rescue them. And that's when the three Israelites responded with the statement above. Look at their words again. It might be the most courageous statement of faith anyone has ever uttered.

It's one thing to say, "I will obey God because I know he's going to protect me." It's a whole different ballgame to say, "I'm going to obey God even if he allows me to burn to death." That's the kind of extreme faith that leaves a lasting impression on everyone who witnesses it. (Look at the effect it had on Nebuchadnezzar in Daniel 3:28-29.)

That's the kind of extreme faith God uses to produce miracles. Do you think you have that kind of faith? Are you ready to put yourself on the line for God's sake—without knowing how things will turn out?

For the fiery account of Shadrach, Meshach, and Abednego's courageous stand, look at Daniel 3:1-30.

 **Fire Away**

If Shadrach, Meshach, and Abednego had been jokers, they might have taunted the Babylonians from the furnace with comments like these:

- "Send in some hot dogs and marshmallows!"
- "Could you throw a couple more logs on the fire? It's getting a little chilly in here."
- "Is this your way of firing us?"
- "Fire in the hole!"
- "How about a little water? Let's get a sauna going!"
- "Somebody pass me the ball. I'm *en fuego*!"
- "Do you smell something burning?"
- "How would you like us—rare, medium, or well done?"

Guaranteed Freshness

Because of the LORD's great love we are not consumed, for his compassions never fail. They are new every morning; great is your faithfulness.

Lamentations 3:22-23

"Everybody Hurts." That's the title of an old R.E.M. song. If the band had been looking to do a theme album, they might have included tracks with titles such as "Everybody Fails," "Everybody Doubts," "Everybody Fears," and "Everybody Gives Up."

You'll notice the common word in all of those titles is *everybody*.

One of the worst things about struggling with your emotions is the loneliness it creates. You convince yourself that you are completely alone in your struggles. That no one else experiences the things you experience. That other people are too strong, too spiritually mature, or too together to ever be dragged down by the kind of emotions that plague you. But that's not true.

Every believer faces times when life seems overwhelming—even pointless. Times when you can't get excited about the thought of facing another day. Times when you wonder where you'll get the strength to carry on. That's why every believer clings equally hard to the promise of Lamentations 3:22-23.

One of God's greatest gifts to us is his daily gift of grace. Notice how his blessings are described: "new *every* morning." That means no matter how much of his grace and blessings you needed yesterday, there's a fresh, unlimited supply ready for you today. So it's safe to say your troubles will never outnumber his blessings. And because of God's unbelievable love for you, you never have to worry about your struggles overwhelming you. If you will ask him, he will give you the strength, motivation, and encouragement you need to make it through the day ahead—no matter what the day may bring.

Remember, this isn't about your strength—it's about God's. And his strength is constantly available to you. So what is there to worry about?

For more of Jeremiah's unique perspective on God, check out Lamentations 3:1-66.

 ## Five Things You Wish Were New Every Day

1. The car you drive to school.

2. The test you bombed yesterday.

3. The clothes you wear.

4. The leftovers in your refrigerator.

5. The last day of the school year.

Loyalty to the King

Saul died because he was unfaithful to the LORD; he did not keep the word of the LORD and even consulted a medium for guidance, and did not inquire of the LORD. So the LORD put him to death and turned the kingdom over to David son of Jesse.

1 Chronicles 10:13-14

"Saul died because he was unfaithful to the Lord." As epitaphs go, that's about as sad as it gets. What a waste.

At one time, Saul seemed to have it all. The honor of having been handpicked by God himself. Immense popularity and respect as Israel's very first human king. Entire armies to help him carry out God's plan. Servants to make his life easier.

Yet Saul had a fatal flaw. He couldn't stay faithful to God. He was constantly looking for something...else. Something more exciting. Something more comforting. Something more dangerous. When God's way didn't suit him, he went his own way.

And he paid the price. Saul learned the hard way that God does not tolerate unfaithfulness. He expects husbands to be faithful to their wives. He expects friends to be faithful to each other. And he especially expects his people to be faithful to him.

Where do you think you rate on the faithfulness scale? If you heard people making fun of your best friend, would you stand up for him or would you keep your mouth shut? If your friend did something that made him seriously unpopular at school, would you stick by him or would you try to separate yourself from him?

More importantly, how faithful are you to God? If you heard a science teacher claim that God doesn't exist, would you stand up for God or would you keep your mouth shut? If identifying yourself as a Christian could make you seriously unpopular with your school crowd, would you stick with God or would you try to hide your relationship with him?

The decision is yours. Will you commit yourself to God's ways? Or will you go your own way?

For the full story of Saul's death, check out 1 Chronicles 10:1-14.

 ## Underwhelming Epitaphs

First Chronicles 10:13 is a pretty disappointing epitaph for a guy like Saul who had such a strong start. Here are some other underwhelming epitaphs:

1. He was always heavy for his age.

2. He preferred root beer to cola.

3. He was not as obnoxious as most people thought.

4. He never cared much for cats.

5. He had no overdue library books at the time of his death.

6. He was never convicted of a felony.

7. He almost fit 88 marshmallows in his mouth at once...and probably should have stopped at 87.

Up and At 'Em

Very early in the morning, while it was still dark, Jesus got up, left the house and went off to a solitary place, where he prayed.

Mark 1:35

Have you ever used the word *radical* to describe prayer?

Don't fall for the myth that prayer is a gentle, sedate, boring responsibility that all Christians have to endure. Prayer is the opportunity to grab the ear of God and talk to your heart's content. About anything and everything. Prayer is the chance to enlist the most powerful Friend in the world to help you—no matter what you're facing. Prayer is the opportunity to have your most nagging questions addressed. Prayer is the chance of a lifetime. And you'd have to be a fool not to wring it for all it's worth.

If you're ready to boost the power of your prayer life, you'll find a couple of helpful tips in the passage above. If anyone understood the radical nature of prayer, it was Jesus. Notice the time of day he chose for his conversation with God. *Very early in the morning.* Jesus couldn't wait to get started.

Do you feel that way about your prayer time? Have you tried setting aside a time early in the day for prayer? You don't necessarily have to get up before dawn, but if you make prayer the first thing you do after you wake up, you'll be a whole lot better prepared to face the challenges of the day.

Notice also the way Jesus protected his time with God. He secluded himself in a place where nothing could interrupt his train of thought. He wanted his entire focus to be on his heavenly Father.

What steps can you take to follow his example? Do you know of a place where you can be alone—away from interruptions and distractions? The good thing about prayer is that you can do it anywhere—a closet, the shower, or even in a car. (Just don't close your eyes if you're driving!)

For a snapshot of Jesus' early ministry, read through Mark 1:1-45.

 ## Common Excuses for Not Getting Up Before Dawn to Pray

- "If I don't get 12 hours of sleep a night, I'm a wreck."
- "I prefer the crack of noon to the crack of dawn."
- "I didn't know there was such a thing as 5 *a.m.*"
- "I don't go to bed until 1 a.m.!"
- "I'm a slave to my body clock."
- "I'm not Jesus."
- "I don't have anything that important to tell God."
- "If God wanted me to be praying at sunrise, he would have made the sun rise later in the day."

What Did You Expect?

I have seen something else under the sun: The race is not to the swift or the battle to the strong, nor does food come to the wise or wealth to the brilliant or favor to the learned; but time and chance happen to them all.

Ecclesiastes 9:11

Someone once said, "If you want to make God laugh, tell him your plans." The fact is, only God knows what the future holds. Therefore he's the only one who can talk with confidence about it. We have no control over what the future holds. Therefore our plans are really nothing more than hopes.

But that shouldn't stop you from looking ahead. A plan that might change in the future is still better than no plan at all. Without plans and goals, you're doomed to drift aimlessly, never really settling on any particular course of action. And that's no way to live.

We will emphasize, though, that counting on your plans to go exactly as you intend is a setup for disappointment. Life is full of unexpected twists and turns—some of them good, some not so good. Over the course of time, some plans get wrecked. Some goals prove unattainable—especially those that are out of your control. Some ambitions turn out to be pipe dreams.

If you're not prepared for those possibilities, you may get discouraged or angry. In some cases, you might even start thinking of yourself as a failure. And that would be a tremendous mistake. You see, God has big plans for you. And regardless of what happens to your plans, his plans won't fail. You can bank on that.

The problem is that God doesn't always reveal his plans to us. At least not completely. That's where faith comes in. In the meantime, the best way to plan for life's ups and downs is to learn to be flexible and creative. If your old plan gets shot down by unexpected circumstances, come up with a new one and keep moving forward. And trust God to keep clearing your path and directing your steps.

To learn more about what the Bible says about destiny, check out Ecclesiastes 9:1-12.

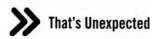 **That's Unexpected**

Sure it's a good idea to expect the unexpected. But some unexpected things are just too far-fetched to consider. Like the following statements—that you won't be hearing again anytime soon:

- "That *Sports Illustrated* swimsuit model thinks you're cute."

- "Here's the money I borrowed from you yesterday."

- "Son, your mother and I have decided that setting a curfew for you is a bad idea. So from now on, you're free to stay out as long as you want—even on school nights."

- "If you haven't started on your term paper yet, don't worry about it. You don't have to do a thing to get an A+. I like to reward procrastinators."

- "I'm sorry I pulled you over, sir. I thought you were speeding, but now I realize that my radar gun was probably wrong. Please accept my apologies. And feel free to squeal your tires and spray gravel all over my car when you pull out."

- "I don't think I pay you enough for the work you do around here. So I've doubled your salary."

The Write Stuff

Tell it to your children, and let your children tell it to their children,
and their children to the next generation.

Joel 1:3

The prophet Joel had some bad news for the Israelites. But rather than trying to soften the blow as much as he could, Joel did the opposite. He commanded the people of Judah to pay close attention to his message. He wanted them to hear every terrible detail of God's impending judgment. He wanted them to know exactly what was coming and why.

Joel wasn't being cruel. He was trying to prevent a repeat of God's judgment in the future. He wanted the people of Judah to share their story with their children so none of them would forget the difficult lesson they were being taught. He figured the children would learn from their parents' mistakes.

Of course, mistakes aren't the only teaching tools available to God's followers. We can also learn from each other's successes and blessings. Hearing about how God intervened in someone else's messed-up circumstances gives hope to other people who aren't sure what the future holds.

What do you think people can learn from your Christian experience so far? What kind of stories will you have to tell your kids and grandkids? What will you warn them about? What will you want to make sure they remember?

Perhaps the best thing you can do for yourself—and anyone else who wants to learn from you—is to start keeping a journal. Develop a habit of writing about what you've seen God do and what you've learned. Be specific. Don't try to gloss over situations or feelings that make you look bad. Remember, the more honest and open you are, the more likely it is someone else will learn from you.

And don't be afraid to share your journaling experiences. Take advantage of the amazing opportunities God gives you to impact the lives of other people—some of whom you may not even know yet.

To see an example of how David journaled about his feelings, read Psalms 23 and 30.

 ## Excerpts from Famous Journals

From Adam:
Fell asleep early yesterday. Don't know why. Just got really tired all of a sudden. When I woke up, my side felt a little weird. But you should have seen what was waiting for me! God called her "woman." Remember when I wrote that the peacock was the most beautiful creature God made? WRONG!

From Joseph:
Had another dream last night. Same as the last one. It ended up with my brothers' symbols bowing down to mine. Cool, huh? I can't wait to tell them about it.

From Moses:
These Israelites are driving me nuts! If one more person asks me why God led us into the desert to die, I swear I'm going to hit something—or someone (ha, ha).

From Jonah:
You're not going to believe where I'm writing this journal entry...Oh, man, it stinks in here...I'm not sure how this is going to end, but I can think of only three ways. Either I'll stay here until I die, or I'll be leaving here by one of two ways. And I don't like any of the options!

Be on Your Toes

The Lord said to Abram, "Leave your country, your people and your father's household and go to the land I will show you."

Genesis 12:1

Pack up everything you own. Kiss your family goodbye. Say *adios* to your friends and neighbors. And move to a foreign country. A place where you know no one. A place where you probably won't be welcome. A place where you'll have to start your life all over again.

Now *that's* a tough assignment.

But Abram didn't complain. He didn't beg for extra time with his loved ones. He didn't even ask God for travel plans. Instead, according to Genesis 12:4, "Abram left, as the Lord had told him."

God commanded and Abram obeyed. Abram turned his comfortable life upside down and launched himself into the unknown, all because of one command and one promise from God. And what did that get Abram? A place of honor in God's eyes, and a place of honor as the father of the Jewish and Arab nations. Check out the "Faith Hall of Fame" in Hebrews 11, the list of people who found favor in God's eyes because of their faithfulness. Abram's (or Abraham's) story of faith is in there with all the others.

God may never move you to a foreign country as he did Abram, but he will move you out of your comfort zone. You can count on that. Whether that means starting a friendship with an outcast at school, taking an unpopular stand on a controversial issue, or sharing your faith in Jesus with someone unexpected, you've got to be ready to obey

God's call when it comes. If you have the faith—and the guts—to show the same kind of extreme obedience that Abram showed, you can expect to find a place of honor in God's eyes, too.

Living faithfully for God is like being an on-duty firefighter. You never know when you're going to get a call, so you have to be ready at all times.

Find the story of God's call and Abram's response in Genesis 12:1-9.

 **The Name Game**

Later in the Genesis story, God changed Abram's name to *Abraham*. He changed Abraham's wife's name from Sarai to *Sarah*. What if he had done the same to other Bible characters?

- Adam might have become Adamham.

- Samson's lover Delilah might have become Delili.

- Noah's son Ham might have become Hamaham.

- Joseph's brother Judah might have become Judi.

- The prophet Elijah might have become Eliji.

- The Old Testament writer Haggai might have become Haggah.

- Joshua might have become Joshui.

- Pharaoh, the king of Egypt, might have become Phari.

- The Israelite judge Deborah might have become Debi.

- Moses' father Amram might have become Amramaham.

Feel free to add your own revised Bible names to the list.

>>

SECTION 4

When Things Get Tough...

Prepare for War

Then the peoples around them set out to discourage the people of Judah and make them afraid to go on building.

Ezra 4:4

The conflict was a simple one. The people of Judah wanted to rebuild the temple in Jerusalem, and their enemies wanted to stop them. So it boiled down to a battle of wills. The side that was most determined to accomplish its goal would emerge victorious. (If you keep reading in the book of Ezra, you'll discover who won. Hint: The winners celebrated their victory in the temple.)

Whether you realize it or not, you face the same kind of conflict in your Christian walk. You are in a battle—a spiritual battle. Your goal is to obey God's commands and follow his will for your life. Satan's goal is to stop you from doing that.

By any means necessary.

Don't be naive. Satan's not going to lie down and let you do God's work without a fight. He's going to throw everything he's got at you. That includes seemingly innocent distractions like friends, girls, sports, and hobbies that can take up too much of your time. But it can also include temptations, doubt, fear, boredom, and anything else that might throw you off course. If you're not prepared to deal with whatever obstacles come your way, you're in trouble.

Fortunately for you, you're teamed up with the one who knows exactly what's coming your way. And when. And while he may not always give you a lot of advance warning, he will always prepare you for it. If you ask him.

Nothing their enemies did could stop the people of Judah from completing God's work. And the same holds true for you today. If you'll focus on doing God's work, nothing will be able to stand in your way. At least not for very long. The key is to keep hammering away, to keep ignoring distractions, and to keep looking to God for help.

To find out more about how to fight in spiritual warfare, read Ephesians 6:10-18.

 Not-So-Helpful Battle Equipment

(Freely adapted from Ephesians 6:10-18)

- The face mask of fear
- The shin guard of cynicism
- The chest protector of ego
- The bubble wrap of busyness
- The ear muffs of doubt
- The mouth guard of hunger
- The truss of boredom
- The running shoes of cowardice

Going the Distance

Sanballat and Geshem sent me this message: "Come, let us meet together in one of the villages on the plain of Ono." But they were scheming to harm me; so I sent messengers to them with this reply: "I am carrying on a great project and cannot go down. Why should the work stop while I leave it and go down to you?"

Nehemiah 6:2-3

Think about your physical endurance. Can you run a mile without stopping? Five miles? How far can you swim or skate without a break? What about your mental toughness? How long can you put up with people doubting you, questioning the things you do, or trying their hardest to make you fail? That's what you're up against when you sign on to do God's work.

Nehemiah and the people of Judah found that out when they returned to Jerusalem to rebuild the walls around the city. Nehemiah's enemies set up an elaborate scheme to coax him to a meeting where they planned to ambush him. God gave Nehemiah the wisdom to see through his enemies' plot, and he managed to stay out of harm's way. So his enemies tried again. And again. Five times they attempted to lure Nehemiah into a trap. And five times he avoided them.

When that didn't work, the enemies threatened to tell the king of Babylon that the people of Judah were building the wall as part of a plan to revolt against the Babylonians. That would have brought the wrath of the Babylonian army down on the people of Judah. But Nehemiah recognized a scare tactic when he saw one. So instead of panicking, he asked God for the strength to finish the job. And the wall construction continued to completion.

Nehemiah's enemies were determined to stop God's work, no matter how long it took. But they didn't count on Nehemiah's endurance. He simply outlasted them. You, too, can outlast any opposition you may be feeling to your faith. You just need to remind yourself that the Christian life is a marathon, not a sprint. The better your endurance is, the more successful you'll be in your kingdom work.

For Nehemiah's response to the enemies who tried to stop the wall construction, take a look at Nehemiah 6:1-7:3.

 Nine Things That Are Hard to Endure

1. The guy sitting next to you on the team bus who sings "The Wheels on the Bus Go Round and Round"...both to and from the game.

2. A haircut with dull scissors.

3. Your four-year-old niece or nephew who tells you the same knock-knock joke over and over and over and over again.

4. Televised golf tournaments.

5. A *looooong* sermon on a beautiful Sunday morning when you're just dying to get outside.

6. Getting fitted for a suit on a really hot day.

7. A root canal...without anesthesia.

8. Fourth-period history class...without anesthesia.

9. Liver-and-onions night at the dinner table.

Raising Your Game

But Jonah ran away from the LORD and headed for Tarshish. He went down to Joppa, where he found a ship bound for that port. After paying the fare, he went aboard and sailed for Tarshish to flee from the LORD.

Jonah 1:3

God gave Jonah a tough job, no question about it. The idea of taking God's message to the evil Ninevites probably turned Jonah's stomach. And that's what he should have told God. If Jonah had confessed his feelings, God would have helped him work through them. And everything would have ended the way God intended.

But apparently Jonah wasn't the type to confront his issues head on. He didn't even *attempt* to do what he was told. He took off, hoping to outrun God's will for his life. He found out the hard way that no one can run—or swim—fast enough to get away from God.

Imagine the suffering Jonah would have been spared if he'd said, "Lord, I'm not sure I have the strength to carry out this assignment—and I don't even know if I understand what you're trying to do here—but I'm going to give it a try." You can bet God would have supplied him with all of the knowledge, understanding, and courage he needed.

But Jonah chose the hard way. He resisted God's instructions.

Don't make the same mistake. When God speaks to you—whether it's in prayer or through the words of your pastor, youth leader, or the Bible itself—treat it seriously. Don't blow it off. Don't choose to go your own way and do your own thing.

Instead ask God to equip you for the job ahead. If you lack courage, ask him for some. If you lack understanding, ask for clearer vision. If you lack know-how, ask him for a mentor. If you commit yourself to carrying out his will, God will supply your needs.

Jonah found that out a little late. But you don't have to.

For a reminder that God will help you when you need it, read Philippians 4:4-7,19.

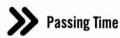 Passing Time

Three days in the belly of a fish is a long time. How did Jonah pass the time?

- Making up offensive names for the Ninevites.

- Throwing himself back and forth against the fish's intestines, trying to give it indigestion.

- Singing "The Stuck-in-the-Belly-of-a-Fish Blues."

- Trying to guess what else the fish had eaten, based on smell and touch.

- Imagining the nicknames people would give him if and when he ever got out of his fishy predicament.

- Boning up on fish anatomy.

- Playing tic-tac-toe on the fish's stomach lining.

- Staying as far away from the fish's colon as possible.

Unstoppable

*This is what I covenanted with you when you came out of Egypt.
And my Spirit remains among you. Do not fear.*

Haggai 2:5

The enemies of Israel couldn't stop the Jewish builders from finishing God's temple. For one simple reason. God was with the builders. And God's side is always the overwhelming favorite to come out on top.

That doesn't always seem like the case, does it? Especially if you've faced more than your share of personal setbacks as a result of being on God's side. Let's face it; it's not always easy to follow God's instructions. In fact, there's usually a price to be paid for it. But here's what we need to understand: Paying that price is not the same as suffering a defeat. The Israelite builders had to deal with the lies and threats of their enemies. That was the price they had to pay. But that price paled in comparison to the ultimate success they enjoyed.

That same ultimate success awaits you—if you're serious about following God's will. Nothing can prevent you from doing what God wants to do. People may try to distract you or put obstacles in your way, but if you're focused on your work, their efforts to stop you or steer you off course will fail.

Let's say God's Holy Spirit gives you the idea to start a lunchtime Bible study at school. Depending on the atmosphere in your community, you may face all kinds of opposition. For example, lawyers who argue that a Bible study violates separation-of-church-and-state laws. Or school board members who refuse to allow you to meet on campus. Or other students who hang around and make life miserable for Bible study members.

Any of these oppositions could cause you headaches in your quest to accomplish God's will. But do not fear, God says. None of them can stop God's long-term plans. He will make sure of that.

For more of God's assuring words to his people, check out Haggai 2:1-9.

Clues That You Might Be Dealing with Someone Who Opposes God's Work

1. He snarls and growls every time Scripture is read.

2. You tell him you plan to design computer games after you graduate; he tells you he plans to oppose God's work.

3. He mentions that he's going to name his first child "Herod," after his favorite Bible character.

4. He often wears a T-shirt that reads, "I [heart] the Edomites."

5. Whenever you try to share your testimony, he covers his ears and chants, "La, la, la, I'm not listening to you."

6. Someone calls him a Philistine, and he takes it as a compliment.

7. He drives a car with a bumper sticker that reads, "I Don't Brake for Christians."

Staring Down Your Fears

Surely God is my salvation; I will trust and not be afraid. The LORD, the LORD, is my strength and my song; he has become my salvation.

Isaiah 12:2

What are your biggest fears? Embarrassing yourself in public? Getting stuck in a tight space? Being left alone? Getting beaten up by a bully? Getting dumped by your girlfriend? Don't try to tell yourself that you're not afraid of anything. Everybody has fears and phobias.

Think about the last time you had to face one of your major fears. How did you react? Maybe you freaked or froze up. Maybe you went to extreme lengths to escape it. Maybe you tried to keep a brave face in front of other people but then lost your composure later? Different people respond to their fears in different ways. The good news is that no matter what your fears are, God can help you work through them.

The prophet Isaiah learned that firsthand. As a prophet with an unpopular message, Isaiah faced more than his share of scary situations. Yet God protected him every step of the way. And the verse above is Isaiah's testimony.

You'll notice, though, that Isaiah doesn't say God will snap his fingers and make your fears instantly go away. That's not the way God works. He wants you to depend on him in every situation—especially when you're scared.

So if you're nervous about, say, speaking in front of a crowd, God won't suddenly make you the world's most confident and gifted public speaker. Instead he will give you the strength you need to get through your speech sentence by sentence. *If* you will put your confidence in him.

Once you learn to trust God with your fears, you may notice yourself becoming bolder and more adventurous. You may find yourself doing things you couldn't have imagined doing a year ago.

See for yourself. Give your fears to God and let him lead you through them...one step at a time.

For more words of strength and courage, check out Isaiah 12:1-6.

 ## Little-Known Fears

- fee-fie-phobia: the fear of the giant in "Jack and the Beanstalk"

- heigh-ho-phobia: the fear of going off to work with seven little people

- hobophobia: the fear of transients

- kokomophobia: the fear of an old Beach Boys song

- locomophobia: the fear of steam engines

- hohohophobia: the fear of guys dressed like Santa Claus

- slowmophobia: the fear of instant replay

- hojophobia: the fear of eating at a Howard Johnson's restaurant

- oboesolophobia: the fear of a solitary woodwind player

- oreophobia: the fear of cream filling

It's Time for a Comeback!

Barnabas wanted to take John, also called Mark, with them, but Paul did not think it wise to take him, because he had deserted them in Pamphylia and had not continued with them in the work.

Acts 15:37-38

Whatever happened to John Mark? This was the guy whose desertion split up Paul and Barnabas, one of the greatest missionary partnerships in Christian history. It's a question worth considering. When you fail on that big of a stage, it's bound to have an impact on your life.

One possibility is that John Mark let his failure ruin his life. That he felt so bad about splitting up Paul and Barnabas, he left Christian ministry forever. That he drifted from place to place, never really forming any meaningful relationships. That he considered himself a loser for the rest of his life.

Does that seem plausible? Think about it. You probably know someone whose life took a terrible turn after a personal failure—whether it was a breakup (or divorce) or an arrest or something else. But that's not how John Mark's story ends. We don't know a lot about the guy, but we do know two things for certain.

First, at the end of Paul's life—when he was imprisoned in a cold dungeon, facing execution, and needed comfort from his closest friends—he asked Timothy to visit him. And to bring with him one person, someone Paul considered helpful in his ministry, *John Mark.* The Bible doesn't give us any details, but apparently somewhere along the way, John Mark made up for his failure and redeemed himself in Paul's eyes (2 Timothy 4:11).

Second, we know that God chose John Mark to write a book about the life of his Son, Jesus. You can find it in your Bible—the second book of the New Testament. The Gospel of Mark.

Take a lesson from the life of John Mark. Remember that failure is not fatal in God's eyes. No matter how badly you blow it, God can—and will—offer you another chance to serve him.

To find out more about overcoming, read through Romans 8:28-39.

 ## John Mark Was Here?

We know John Mark caused Paul and Barnabas to end their partnership. But we don't know much else about his life (other than his writing the Gospel of Mark). His failures could have been worse. Imagine if he had...

- given directions to Judas Iscariot and the rest of the mob to help them find Jesus in the Garden of Gethsemane (see John 18:1-11).

- served as financial advisor to Ananias and Sapphira (see Acts 5:1-11).

- heckled Stephen during his speech to the Sanhedrin (see Acts 7:1-8:1).

- worked as a promoter for Simon the Sorcerer (see Acts 8:9-25).

- told Peter to stop mingling with Gentiles (see Acts 10:1-48).

- given Eutychus a couple of sleeping pills before Paul's upper-room meeting (see Acts 20:7-12).

- passed messages among the conspirators who planned to kill Paul (see Acts 23:12-22).

Fierce Warfare

Be self-controlled and alert. Your enemy the devil prowls around like a roaring lion looking for someone to devour.

1 Peter 5:8

If this description of the devil doesn't rattle you, it should. Don't make the mistake of underestimating your enemy. The devil is a guerilla fighter. He's not bound by the rules of the Geneva Convention. He will use anything—absolutely anything—to destroy your faith and damage your relationship with Christ. Nothing is too low for him.

If he knocks you down, he's not going to walk away and celebrate. He's going to kick you—again and again and again. He'll try to keep you down. You see, Satan isn't trying merely to defeat you. He wants to devour you. He wants to take you out of the picture completely. He wants to get you so frustrated by your weaknesses...so involved in pursuing your own desires...or so distracted by trivial things that you can't live the kind of life Christ calls you to. He wants to eliminate the possibility of your making a difference in this world.

And he'll start by exploiting your weaknesses.

Where are you most vulnerable to Satan's attacks? What temptations seem hardest for you to resist? It's important to know your weak areas if you're going to be on your guard. If you're surfing the Web, maybe you need to take extra care to avoid porn sites. If you struggle with anger, Satan may try to use a couple of really bad days in a row to get you primed for an explosion. So you need to be mentally prepared for that. At the same time, it's equally important not to drop your guard in other areas—no matter how strong you may feel. You may be surprised by what Satan can do with even the slightest opportunity.

Keep your guard up. Stay close to God. And always be ready to fight your enemy.

For more wise advice from the apostle Peter, check out 1 Peter 5:1-11.

 ## The Roaring Lion

The apostle Peter gives us an unforgettable description of Satan as a roaring lion. But perhaps that image came to him only after several previous attempts. Here are some other animal-related images that Peter might have tried and rejected.

"Your enemy the devil prowls around like a..."

- demonic aardvark.
- smooth-running jaguar.
- venomous spider.
- hungry, hungry hippo.
- barbecued chicken.
- cranky crocodile.
- sonic hedgehog.

Can You Handle the Truth?

*So then, brothers, stand firm and hold to the teachings we passed on to you,
whether by word of mouth or by letter.*

2 Thessalonians 2:15

Once you learn the truth of God's Word, you need to prepare yourself to defend that truth against an onslaught of doubters and critics. You'll find that people will try to chip away at the believability of your Christian faith. They'll ask things like, "If God is so loving, how can he send people to hell?" or "Don't you think it's narrow-minded to believe that Jesus is the *only* way to God?" or "How do you know the Bible is true?"

That's not to say there's anything wrong with sincere questioning. The fact is, God welcomes it. He knows his truth can withstand any scrutiny.

The problem comes when sincere questions are met with silence or insufficient answers. If you're prepared to answer tough questions about Christianity and the Bible, you'll find you have a great weapon to defend against the doubts of unbelievers. Not only will your own faith be strengthened, you will also help the seeking spirits of those asking the questions. Or that of other unbelievers who overhear your exchange.

That's one reason why you need to continue to learn more about being a Christian. Obviously that takes a long time, but it can happen. Tons of great books have been written about how to defend the Christian faith and how to answer tough questions about it. You can find them online, in your local Christian bookstore, or maybe even in your church library.

You can also gain expertise by talking to your parents (if they're Christians), your pastor, your youth leader, or other mature believers about questions they've been asked. You can learn not only from their effective defenses of the faith but also from their mistakes.

Don't be intimidated by this responsibility. Remember, God rewards commitment. The more effort you put into becoming an expert on God's Word, the more confidence and wisdom he will give you.

Learn more about how to stand firm in your faith from 2 Thessalonians 2:13-17.

 ## Questions You Don't Have to Worry About

Some Bible-related questions may present a real challenge to your faith. Here are some that probably won't:

- Why didn't Titus get a second letter from Paul?

- What if a man builds his primary residence on rock, but builds a vacation home on sand—is he wise or foolish?

- Did it bother the disciples to know they could never call in sick to work (because Jesus just would have healed them on the spot)?

- Do you suppose any of Noah's sons went into the fertilizer business after all that time in the ark?

True or False

If a liar and deceiver comes and says, "I will prophesy for you plenty of wine and beer," he would be just the prophet for this people!

Micah 2:11

Do you know how law-enforcement officials learn to spot counterfeit money? They study real money. They pore over every detail of the genuine article, memorizing what it looks like, how it feels, how it responds under certain conditions. They become so familiar with the real thing that it doesn't take them long to figure out when they're dealing with a counterfeit.

If you're a Christian who's serious about guarding yourself against false teachers, you might want to consider the same approach. The more you know about the Bible—what it says and what it doesn't say—the better equipped you'll be to spot phony philosophies and faulty spiritual teaching.

You can find warnings against false teachers throughout the Old and New Testaments. It was a problem God took very seriously. And he still does. Unfortunately, spotting false teachers isn't an easy thing to do. Most false teachers don't say things that are obviously false. They sprinkle just enough biblical truth in with their teachings to make them sound legitimate (for example, "Jesus is one path to God"). Or they twist one element of an accepted biblical truth to create something unacceptable (for example, "God is a loving Creator...who will not allow any of his creation to suffer for eternity").

Recognizing biblical errors in a teacher's words requires effort—not to mention an understanding of God's truth. If you're not paying careful attention, you may end up believing something you shouldn't.

And God will hold you accountable for it. Yes, false teachers will be punished for their lies. But you'll have to answer to God for the lies you fall for—and for failing to defend his truth.

Are you up for the challenge? Are you familiar enough with God's Word to be able to spot counterfeit teachings? If not, what steps can you take to become a vigilant defender of God's truths?

For more of God's harsh words against false teachers, check out Micah 2:6-11.

Easy Ways to Recognize a False Teacher

Wouldn't it be great if spotting a false teacher were this simple?

1. He insists *The Lord of the Rings* trilogy is in the Old Testament.

2. He refuses to teach while hooked up to a polygraph.

3. He refers to angels as "Casper."

4. He insists Jesus was a Pennsylvanian—born in Bethlehem and raised in Nazareth.

5. He pronounces the "P" in Psalms.

6. When you mention Jesus' resurrection, he says he's not familiar with the story.

7. His list of Jesus' 12 disciples includes Abraham, Moses, and a guy named Chuck.

8. He mentions a prequel to the book of Genesis.

SECTION 6

Peer Pressure

No Pain, No Gain

At that time the Lord said to Joshua, "Make flint knives and circumcise the Israelites again."

Joshua 5:2

Most circumcisions take place shortly after birth—before nerve endings become fully sensitized. And while it's still not a pleasant experience for the baby, it's a lot less painful than it is for an adult who undergoes the procedure.

That's why the Israelite men must have cringed when they got word of God's command to be circumcised. This was a sign of God's covenant with them. God wanted to make sure that they were fully committed to him. That was a price the Israelites had to pay for being God's chosen people. And considering everything God did for them, it was a small price to pay. (Although you might have had a hard time convincing the newly circumcised guys of that.)

What about you? Have you ever had to pay a price for following God? Have you ever been made fun of for the things you believe? Have you ever been left off a party invitation list because of the things you refuse to put in your body? Have you ever been misunderstood because of the way you live? Have you ever been verbally attacked for taking a moral stand?

A good rule of thumb to remember is that if obeying God seems painless to you, you're probably not doing it as well as you should. You see, God's will often contradicts the way our society says we should live. If you're serious about following God, you're going to stand out—often in uncomfortable ways. You're going to bother some people. You're going to make them think about things they'd rather not think about. You're going to set yourself up as a target for jokes and abuse.

But at least you'll be assured of two things. One, that God will ultimately reward your faithfulness. And two, that you'll have an easier time than the Israelite men did at Gibeath Haaraloth. Yowsa!

For more on God's uncomfortable command to the Israelite men, look at Joshua 5:1-10.

 Five Things You Don't Want to Hear after You've Just Been Circumcised

1. "Mount your horses. We've got a 50-mile ride ahead of us."

2. "Everybody ready for stretching exercises and jumping jacks?"

3. "Someone stole all your linen clothes. I'm afraid you're going to have to wear sackcloth underwear."

4. "We've prepared a vat of iodine for you to soak in."

5. "Oops, looks like I cut the wrong part. We're going to have to try it again."

Break Away

This is what the Lord says: "Although they have allies and are numerous, they will be cut off and pass away. Although I have afflicted you, O Judah, I will afflict you no more."

Nahum 1:12

"Come on, everyone else is doing it. You're not going to get in trouble." Under the right circumstances, those words can be pretty persuasive. Even if they involve doing something you know is wrong.

For example, if your friends are getting smashed at a party, doesn't it increase the chances that you're going to drink, too? Or if you know that most of your store coworkers occasionally lift merchandise after hours, doesn't it make you more comfortable with the idea of doing it yourself?

Call it peer pressure or anything you want, but you've got to admit, disobeying God is a lot easier when other people are doing it, too. It's easy to fall into the trap of believing that there's safety in numbers. Or to believe that if your involvement isn't as extreme as someone else's in the group, you're off the hook. And if we're talking about human authority, there might be some basis for those beliefs. But we're not talking about human authority. We're talking about God who sees everything...and who holds every person accountable for the things he or she does. Period.

God doesn't judge people in numbers. He judges us individually. Each of us must stand alone before him to accept individual consequences. He doesn't grade on a sliding scale. He doesn't say, "What you did was wrong, but at least you weren't as bad as that guy." God simply says, "What you did was wrong."

That's why, for Christians, being part of the crowd is a dangerous position. It can give us a false sense of security—not to mention a false sense of right and wrong. Remember, God calls us to separate ourselves from the crowd. To follow him as an individual. To let him determine right and wrong for us.

Are you up for the challenge?

To see how Jesus stood up against the crowd, read John 2:12-24 and John 7.

Nine Ways to Be Really Different

There's different...and then there's *really* different. Here are nine ways to achieve the latter status:

1. Wear orange shoes...all the time.

2. Burst into a chorus of "I did it my way" three or four times a day for no apparent reason.

3. Greet everyone you encounter with the phrase, "What's up, Ringo?"

4. Wear a clown nose to school every Friday.

5. Use a hacking cough as the ring tone for your phone.

6. Refuse to listen to any music made after 1965.

7. Bow to everyone you encounter.

8. Invite your school's least popular teacher to double-date with you and your girlfriend.

9. Combine steps 3 and 7.

Say Something!

Get yourself ready! Stand up and say to them whatever I command you.
Do not be terrified by them, or I will terrify you before them.

Jeremiah 1:17

Sometimes speaking up is the most dangerous thing you can do. When your words might identify you as someone with a different point of view...someone with unfashionable compassion...or someone who's looking for confrontation, the temptation to keep your mouth shut is intense. After all, there's safety in remaining quiet.

In most cases, silence is the easy way out. However, silence is not always the best option for God's people. You see God's not interested in the easy way out for us. He never promised his followers trouble-free lives. But he does promise to reward obedience. Like the kind of obedience the prophet Jeremiah displayed when he took God's controversial message to the people of Judah. (That's what this entry's verse is all about.)

Do you have the courageous spirit needed to stand up for what's right? When you hear friends talk about bulking up with steroids... or smoking pot on weekends...or treating girls like sex objects, do you ever speak about what Jesus would do? At the very least, are you willing to distance yourself from the kind of lives your friends have chosen? Are you willing to risk losing friendships—and even making some enemies—in order to spread God's truth like Jeremiah did?

It's ironic that the excuse many believers offer for not speaking up is the fear of offending other people. Talk about a misguided point of view! The one we should be worried about offending is the one who commands us to speak up. He makes that clear in Jeremiah 1:17.

God takes obedience seriously. So when the time comes to open your mouth, don't worry about the consequences. Just say what God's told you to say, and let God take care of the rest.

For the full story of God's call to Jeremiah, check out Jeremiah 1:1-19.

 Times When Silence Is Your Best Option

- Attending a mime convention.
- A librarian whispers, "Shhh!"
- You come across a "Danger: Avalanche" sign on a downhill ski run.
- A police officer asks, "Do you have anything you want to say to me?" after he stops you for speeding.
- Tiptoeing through a pen of sleeping lions at the zoo.

Step Up

But Mordecai found out about the plot and told Queen Esther, who in turn reported it to the king, giving credit to Mordecai.

Esther 2:22

Abraham Lincoln once said, "Better to remain silent and be thought a fool than to speak and remove all doubt." Someone else coined the phrase, "Silence is golden." The idea behind both statements is that there's something noble about keeping one's mouth shut. And while you can probably think of several situations in which that's true, there are many other situations in which staying silent is absolutely the worst thing a person can do.

Legally speaking, if you know of someone being picked on or plotted against and you do nothing about it, you're an accomplice to the crime. It's called "being an accessory before the fact" or "reckless indifference," take your pick. Even if you had nothing to do with carrying out the plan, you're still held liable if you could have done something to prevent an attack but didn't.

As Christians our responsibility is even greater. Jesus has given us a spirit of boldness, not fear. He's also given us an example to follow. Think about the many times he spoke against injustice and confronted people who were mistreating others. That's what he wants us to do.

Bullies and people who make life miserable for others rarely stop the abuse on their own. They have to be stopped...by someone like you. We're not talking about becoming a thug or a vigilante, policing the streets for jerks. We're talking about exposing the things that are going on and speaking up about them instead of averting your eyes and refusing to care.

Chances are you know someone who's being bullied, picked on, or plotted against—whether it's at school, in your neighborhood, or at work. Are you prepared to follow Mordecai's example in this entry's verse and speak up about it? Remember God's on your side. What is there to worry about?

For more on being bold, read Ephesians 5:8-20.

 Weird Conspiracies

Mordecai uncovered a conspiracy to assassinate the king of Persia. Here are some even stranger conspiracies you may want to look into:

1. Why does something outrageously memorable happen at every party you're not invited to?

2. Why are toys never as fun in real life as they look on TV?

3. When your local TV station runs the list of cancelled school days due to ice storms or heavy snowfall, why is yours never on that list?

4. Why is the DVD you really want to watch never in stock when you go to the video store?

5. How do zits know to appear on the eve of a big date?

And Then There Was One

But Noah found favor in the eyes of the Lord.

Genesis 6:8

Imagine how weird Noah must have looked to his friends and neighbors. A guy almost 600 years old spending his days building a giant boat and collecting all kinds of animals...for no obvious reason.

Noah must have known when he accepted God's unusual assignment that he was setting himself up to be doubted, questioned, and made fun of. Again and again and again. Maybe that bothered him, maybe it didn't. The Bible doesn't say. But we do know that nothing stopped him from finishing the job.

Noah wasn't looking to find favor in the eyes of his friends and neighbors. He cared only about finding favor in God's eyes. Smart move. If Noah had tried to live his life to please the people around him, he would have been treading water with them when the flood came.

Noah understood a very important spiritual truth. That is, if you're worried about what other people think of you, you can't be an effective part of God's plan. You'll get discouraged or embarrassed too easily. God's work isn't a job for cowards or chameleons—people whose main goal in life is to keep their heads down and blend in with the crowd. The kind of people God uses to accomplish his will are those who are willing to step away from the crowd—away from doing what everyone else is doing—in order to take a bold stand for him.

Does that describe you? Do you have what it takes to be a stand-alone guy? Are you willing to risk losing friends, being labeled a religious freak, or being made fun of for doing what's right? If you want

REVOLUTION DEVOTIONAL

to truly follow God, your place will be out in the open, where everyone knows who you serve.

For the full story of Noah's building project and its results, skim through Genesis 6:1-9:29.

 Top-Ten Complaints of Noah's Neighbors

1. Elephant droppings.

2. Noah's failure to obtain the necessary building permits for the ark.

3. Rhinoceros droppings.

4. Nonstop whistling of "Row, Row, Row Your Boat" during the ark's construction.

5. Hippopotamus droppings.

6. Noah constantly holding up small animals and asking, "Does this look like a male or female to you?"

7. Giraffe droppings.

8. Disappointed cries of the animals not chosen by Noah.

9. Zebra droppings.

10. Decrease in property values, thanks to the giant boat in Noah's front yard.

Are You Ready?

The rest of the people—priests, Levites, gatekeepers, singers, temple servants and all who separated themselves from the neighboring peoples for the sake of the Law of God, together with their wives and all their sons and daughters who are able to understand—all these now join their brothers the nobles, and bind themselves with a curse and an oath to follow the law of God given through Moses the servant of God and to obey carefully all the commands, regulations and decrees of the LORD our Lord.

Nehemiah 10:28-29

Do you want to be just like everybody else, or do you want to stand out from the crowd? Sure, blending in has its advantages. There's not much risk in being just like everybody else. If people don't know where you stand, they can't take potshots at you. If you don't make your beliefs known, you don't have to worry about confrontation. On the other hand, being different is cool, too. There's honor in doing the right thing and being a leader. And don't underestimate the value of honor in your life.

Throughout the Bible, God's call to his people was to be different, "set apart" from other people for himself. He didn't ask this because the Israelites were better than others, or because he wanted to put others down. God required this because he loved them deeply. He asked them to be separate in order to make their faith in the true God visible to the people around them. He wanted them to experience his protection as opposed to the "safety" of fitting in with the crowd. He wanted them on his team, not just concerned about their own individuality.

God's call to be on his separate team continues today, and it's going out to you. It's tough to be different. It's tough to have morals and standards. But the rewards are great. You'll make God look good, and you'll save yourself loads and loads of heartache.

Are you ready to leave the safety of the crowd? Are you ready to be the guy people know is a Christian? Are you ready to speak out against things you know aren't right? Are you ready to make a difference in the world around you? Are you ready to trust God—and God alone—for your safety and protection?

Then what are you waiting for? Ask God for the courage to take a risk and be different from the people around you.

To discover more of how the Jewish exiles were to be different, see Nehemiah 10:28-39.

 Bad Ways to Separate Yourself From the Crowd

- Resolve to eat nothing but baked beans for a week.
- Buy a pet rattlesnake—and take him with you in public.
- Stop showering.
- Ride a tricycle to school every day.
- Wear red contact lenses and stare intensely at anyone who talks to you (make sure you don't blink).
- Stop cutting your hair and your fingernails—for the rest of your life.

Who You Trying to Please?

The messenger who had gone to summon Micaiah said to him, "Look, as one man the other prophets are predicting success for the king. Let your word agree with theirs, and speak favorably." But Micaiah said, "As surely as the LORD lives, I can tell him only what the Lord tells me."

1 Kings 22:13-14

The king of Israel and the king of Judah decided to team up to attack the city of Ramoth Gilead. Before they went into battle, however, they wanted to make sure God was on their side. So they consulted 400 false prophets who all assured them God would give them victory.

But that wasn't good enough for the king of Judah. He wanted to hear from a prophet of the Lord. So the kings sent for Micaiah. The prophet knew the kings expected good news from him. And the easiest solution would have been to tell them what they wanted to hear. But Micaiah wasn't driven by other people's expectations. He was driven by God's expectations.

So he did what he had to do—and paid the price for it. But you can bet his story had a happy ending. Because Micaiah did what God wanted him to do.

Are you a people pleaser by nature? Do you go out of your way to make others happy or avoid confrontation? If so, what has that approach to life gained you? What has it cost you?

Few things in life are more difficult than trying to meet other people's expectations. For one thing, rarely will you have just one set of expectations to think about. Your parents expect one thing from you, your coaches and teachers expect another, your friends expect one thing, and your girlfriend expects yet another. Pleasing everyone is virtually impossible. Trying to do so only makes you miserable. Your best bet, then, is to focus on meeting God's expectations for your life, allowing him to help you deal properly with everyone else's.

And what does God expect from you? He expects you to study his Word. He expects you to obey his commands. And he expects you to live your faith boldly. If you will do those things, you can bet your story will have a happy ending, too.

To read more about how the disciples chose to please God first, read Acts 4.

If You Tried to Meet Everyone's Expectations You'd Be...

- the valedictorian and president of your high school class;
- voted most likely to succeed, most popular, and most likely to marry a supermodel;
- a three-sport college All-American;
- a *summa cum laude* graduate of a prestigious Ivy League school;
- juggling careers as a doctor, a lawyer, and the CEO of a Fortune 500 company;
- playing major league baseball on the side;
- a family man who manages to find time to be home for dinner every night;
- a dad who coaches his kids' soccer, basketball, and baseball teams;
- a devoted husband who whisks his wife away to exotic vacations every month;
- a respected Sunday school teacher;
- the guy responsible for curing cancer *and* baldness;

...but you'd still have to answer Jesus' question in Mark 8:36: "What good is it for a man to gain the whole world, yet forfeit his soul?"

Big Difference

*But because my servant Caleb has a different spirit and follows
me wholeheartedly, I will bring him into the land he went to,
and his descendants will inherit it.*

Numbers 14:24

Here's the story on Caleb. When the Israelites got to the Promised Land
after leaving Egypt, the land was already occupied. If the Israelites wanted it, they were going to have to fight for it. Moses, the leader of the
Israelites, sent 12 spies into the land to get the scoop on their enemies.

Ten of the spies came back with discouraging news. The people
who lived in the land were giants, they said. There's no way we puny
Israelites can defeat them.

Caleb, however, had a different attitude toward the situation—or,
as the book of Numbers describes it, a "different spirit." Caleb's scouting report went something like this: "So what if the people in the land
are big? We have God on our side, and there's nothing he can't do. Let's
let him lead us into the land and do what needs to be done."

Caleb's faith in God gave him the courage to choose a course of
action that was different from what everyone else wanted to do. His
opinion didn't make him popular, that's for sure. But it pleased God.
And that's all that mattered.

Caleb had an *extreme* faith. It wasn't something he simply talked
about. It was something he lived. He refused to allow fear to interfere
with what God wanted him to do. That explains his "different spirit."

What would a guy with a different spirit do today? Would he refuse to join in when his friends started ripping on someone? Would he stand up for someone getting picked on at school? Would he blow off parties where he knew people were going to get wasted? Would he speak up in science class about why he believes God created the universe? Would he invite his non-Christian friends to a youth group activity? What do *you* think he would do to show that he is really set apart?

And here's the most important question of all: Are you willing to be that guy?

For the full story of Caleb's stand against the rest of the Israelite spies, read Numbers 14:1-45.

 ## Seven More Ways to Be Really Different

Earlier in this book, we offered some unconventional ideas for standing out among your peers. Here are some more:

1. Color your eyebrows with a purple magic marker.

2. Insist that people call you "Butterscotch."

3. Wear bumper stickers on the back of your coat.

4. Declare yourself a "meat-arian" and argue for vegetable rights.

5. Talk only in Dr. Seuss rhymes.

6. At the lunch table, do play-by-play commentary for a game going on in your imagination.

7. Randomly blurt out the phrase, "Now *that's* what I'm talking about"—even when no one is talking.

SECTION 6

Where's Your Passion?

With Everything You've Got

I intend, therefore, to build a temple for the Name of the LORD my God, as the LORD told my father David, when he said, "Your son whom I will put on the throne in your place will build the temple for my Name."

1 Kings 5:5

Imagine you're standing by your school locker one morning when the football coach approaches you. He looks you in the eye and tells you he has one spot left on the varsity roster with your name on it—if you're willing to work hard enough to earn it. (If you're not a football guy, substitute your favorite sport. If you're not a sports guy, imagine the producer of your favorite reality TV show offering you a chance to be a contestant.)

You have an incredible opportunity staring you in the face. All you need is the vision, desire, and drive to make it a reality. Would you go for it? How hard would you push yourself? What would you be willing to sacrifice in order to accomplish your goal?

Now what if your golden opportunity was spiritual instead of athletic? Would it lessen your passion? If King Solomon were here, he'd tell you it shouldn't.

Solomon was a man of vision. Like an all-pro running back weaving through defenders, when he saw an opening, he hit it hard. As king, he looked back on all that his father David had wanted to do. He realized that he could accomplish many of those things. So he laid out his objectives, did a little networking, and set his plan in motion.

Are you a young man of vision? Are you a man of passion about God's work? You don't have to build palaces and temples to accomplish something for God. Maybe the opportunity in front of you is a job or a relationship, a leadership role in your church, or a change in your personal devotion to God. Whatever it is, see the opening and go for it. With every bit of passion in you.

To get the details of Solomon's temple-building project, check out 1 Kings 6:1-38.

 ## If You Were Building a Church, What Kind of Features Would You Include?

You've read about what Solomon included in his temple for God. What would you include in your worship center?

- "Magic finger" pews to keep you relaxed and comfortable during the sermon?

- ATMs in the lobby for people who forget their tithes and offerings?

- A retractable roof to let the sun shine in?

- State-of-the-art training facilities for the church softball team?

- Adjoining hotel suites for youth group lock-ins?

- A zero-depth swimming pool that could double as a baptismal?

- Hydraulic stage risers and special effect lasers for the worship musicians?

All Fired Up

*Jehu said, "Come with me and see my zeal for the LORD."
Then he had him ride along in his chariot.*

2 Kings 10:16

If your coach told you that you could get a lot more playing time by working on a few areas of your game, you'd probably bust your tail, wouldn't you? You'd want to show your coach how much heart you've got. You'd want to convince him that you're committed to his program. You'd want to impress him with your attitude and work ethic.

Now, what if God told you that you could gain a bigger role in his plan for the world by developing certain areas of spiritual weakness? How hard would you be willing to work in order to strengthen those areas?

The energy you put into pleasing God and doing his work is called *zeal*. Jehu, the king of Israel, was full of zeal for God. Jehu took the throne about 12 years after the evil king Ahab died. God had vowed through the prophet Elijah to destroy Ahab and his descendants because of Ahab's wickedness. Jehu committed himself to carrying out God's vow by killing all of Ahab's descendants. That's how he showed his zeal for God.

How do we show zeal for God? We get fired up about Bible study. We readily defend the Christian faith. We verbally encourage our Christian friends. We take risks to serve others.

Keep in mind that it's not necessarily your work or what you *do* that God cares about; rather it's your attitude toward your work. And God loves zeal. The more zealous you are, the more your words, actions, and prayers can impact the world for God's glory.

For more on Jehu's zeal for God, look at 2 Kings 10:1-17.

 Bumper Stickers on Jehu's Chariot

- "There's more than one way to get A HEAD in this world."
- "You can run, but you can't hide."
- "Ahab, meet Moby Dick."
- "Go ahead, Ahab supporters, make my day."
- "Keepin' it Jezreel."

Top Priority

But the LORD said to Samuel, "Do not consider his appearance or his height, for I have rejected him. The LORD does not look at the things man looks at. Man looks at the outward appearance, but the LORD looks at the heart."

1 Samuel 16:7

Serious athletes have all kinds of ways of measuring their strength and progress. They can tell you exactly how much weight they can bench-press and squat...how high they can pole-vault...how fast they can run a 40-yard sprint...how hard they can throw a fastball...and how high their vertical leap is.

But how do you measure spiritual growth and progress? God makes it clear that he doesn't really care about how we look on the outside. When he was choosing the king of Israel, he bypassed the older, taller, stronger sons and went for the younger, shorter, scrawny son, David.

One method you can use to measure your spiritual growth is your familiarity with the Bible. How many verses do you know by heart, how much quality time do you spend in God's Word, and how comfortable are you talking about it? The Bible is your means of spiritual nourishment for growing strong.

Another measuring device is your response to setbacks, disappointments, and temptation. Are you spiritually strong enough to avoid physical and emotional meltdowns when things don't go your way? Are you quick to turn situations over to God? Do you pray for his strength? Do you base your decisions on what you think Jesus would do in your situation?

A third measuring stick is the effect your faith is having on the people around you. Have they noticed the changes your faith has made in your life? Are they curious about your commitment to Christ? Do they ask questions? Have their lives been impacted by your walk with God?

Take a moment to think about your priorities. How much time do you spend honing your body, building your muscle mass, and increasing your physical strength? How does that compare with the time you spend honing your relationship with God, increasing your Bible knowledge, and building your spiritual strength? Remember, God isn't terribly interested in how much you can squat or bench-press. He cares about your heart. He cares about how well you resist temptation, how strong your faith remains during tough times, and how you introduce him to others.

Are you ready to bulk up spiritually?

For the account of God's surprising choice of a candidate to be king, check out 1 Samuel 16:1-13.

 Your Athletic Career

Scripture sometimes uses the example of the athlete in getting across spiritual truths. Here are some things you don't want people to know about your athletic career.

- You ride the bench on the freshman football team—and you're a senior.

- You scored the game-winning goal in the championship soccer game—for the other team.

- The only sport you've ever played is botchy ball—and you got injured.

- When you cried to your mom after you skipped first base and ran straight to second while playing in a Little League baseball game.

- When you cried to your mom after you skipped first base and ran straight to second while playing in a varsity high school baseball game.

- The first time you tried the high jump and the pole somehow took down your shorts (and part of your pride as well).

- Your basketball coach let you be on the team just so the other players would feel better about themselves.

- The time you got tangled up with the bench press and couldn't seem to get the thing off your chest (or have enough air in your lungs to call for help).

- The first time you tried to jump a hurdle, didn't quite make it, and screamed like a girl in front of your whole gym class.

The Deepest Satisfaction of All

A man can do nothing better than to eat and drink and find satisfaction in his work. This too, I see, is from the hand of God, for without him, who can eat or find enjoyment?

Ecclesiastes 2:24-25

What kinds of things give you satisfaction? Getting an "A" on a paper you nearly killed yourself to finish? Learning the chords to one of your favorite songs? Increasing your bench-press by 20 pounds?

Whatever it is, give thanks to God for it. The book of Ecclesiastes makes it clear that he's the one who gives true satisfaction and joy.

That may come as a surprise to some people who have a hard time using the words *God* and *satisfaction* in the same sentence. They picture God as a cosmic killjoy, one whose goal is to spoil people's fun. They point to his commands in the Bible as evidence of his unsatisfying nature. They complain about the restrictions he puts on their pursuits of satisfaction. They blame him for their unhappiness.

The problem with that way of thinking is that it mistakes temporary pleasure for genuine satisfaction. Lots of things can give you temporary pleasure. But that doesn't mean they will ultimately satisfy you. King Solomon calls them "meaningless" (Ecclesiastes 2:1). Giving in to your sexual urges (with someone other than your wife) can give you immediate pleasure. But knowing that you spoiled one of God's great gifts won't bring you ultimate satisfaction. (And neither will the guilt, sexually transmitted diseases, or unwanted pregnancies that often go along with it.) Likewise, smoking pot may give you pleasure for a while. But the damage you could do to your brain cells will be a big obstacle in your search for satisfaction.

God made you for himself. He created you to find your deepest satisfaction in knowing and enjoying him. Trying to find this satisfaction anywhere else will do nothing but leave you empty. Why would you want to play around with second best? Resolve to come to God for your fulfillment—the only place it can be found.

For more of King Solomon's thoughts on meaninglessness and satisfaction, check out Ecclesiastes 2:1-26.

 ## Eight Things That Are Unlikely to Bring Satisfaction

1. A paper cut on your tongue.

2. Brussels sprout pudding.

3. A 24-CD box set of an unabridged dictionary read aloud.

4. Watching C-Span for three hours with your date and her parents.

5. A 24-hour bus trip.

6. Three bags full of junk mail.

7. A massage from Captain Hook.

8. Eating poison ivy.

SECTION 7

Relationships

Let It Go!

If we confess our sins, he is faithful and just and will forgive us our sins and purify us from all unrighteousness.

1 John 1:9

God demands one thing from us when we sin: genuine repentance. He wants us to recognize what we've done—how we've hurt our relationships with him and with anyone else who was affected by our sin. He wants us to feel genuine sorrow, and he wants us to come to him in prayer to make things right.

And if we'll do that, he will forgive us.

But God doesn't *just* forgive us. He also purifies us. That means he washes away the sins we confess. He scrubs our hearts clean. And he forgets about our sin forever. That's his promise to us.

Now here's a tip for you: If God forgets about a sin, you should forget about it, too. Don't keep beating yourself up over something you've been forgiven for. Do what you need to do in order to make things right. Apologize to anyone who might have been hurt as a result of your actions. Ask for forgiveness. Fix the situation if you can. And when you're done with that, put the incident behind you—for good—and move on with your life.

Moving on means not allowing other people to keep you down because of something you've done in the past. If someone refuses to forgive and forget after you've sincerely tried to make amends, that's his problem. He'll have to answer to God for his hardened heart. Moving on also means rejecting unfair reputations that people try to give you. Don't allow yourself to be defined by a past mistake.

Remember, if it comes down to a choice of believing what people say about you and believing what God's Word says about you, always go with God's Word.

To learn how to "walk in the light" as a believer, take a look at 1 John 1:5-2:14.

 Signs That Someone Hasn't Truly Forgiven You

1. Begins every conversation with, "Remember that time you hurt me so badly?"

2. Hasn't looked you in the eye since elementary school.

3. Wears a hat that reads, "I haven't forgiven..."—with your name underneath.

4. Breaks into sobs every time you enter the room.

5. Responds to every question you ask with, "Liar says what?"

6. Can't say the words "forgive and forget" without snarling.

7. Has 1 John 1:9 crossed out in his Bible.

Keepin' It Under Control

You used to walk in these ways, in the life you once lived. But now you must rid yourselves of all such things as these: anger, rage, malice, slander, and filthy language from your lips.

Colossians 3:7-8

God's work doesn't stop at salvation. Accepting Christ as your Savior is merely the first step in a long, wonderful transformation that God has in store for you. God doesn't just want to hear you say, "I believe." He wants to change you from the inside out. And he wants to do it in a noticeable way.

Have your friends or family members noticed any differences in you since you became a Christian? If so, what changes have they specifically mentioned? Have their attitudes toward you changed at all? If so, how does that make you feel?

If you became a Christian at an early age, those questions may not apply. (Unless, say, you were a hardened criminal as an eight-year-old.) If that's the case, you need to ask yourself if your Christian faith sets you apart from other people at school, at work, or in your neighborhood. If people haven't noticed a difference in your life, or if you find yourself blending in too easily with unbelievers, you may need to step back and examine your lifestyle choices. God wants his people to stand apart. To be noticeably different from the crowd in the way we talk and the way we act.

That's what the apostle Paul is getting at in the verses above. Anyone can respond to an irritating situation with a violent outburst or with a string of swear words. Anyone can find ways to tear down another person. Anyone can give in to his natural impulses. You don't need God for that.

But the guy who manages to control his anger...who chooses building up people instead of tearing them down...who refuses to let his natural impulses control him...is like a walking billboard, calling attention to God's ability to transform people.

To find out more about what God expects from his followers, read Colossians 3:1-17.

 ## Signs That People Aren't Noticing Changes in Your Life

1. In a car with your friends, you point out your church as you drive past and someone says, "*You* go to church? No way!"

2. Sailors and truck drivers often tell you to watch your language.

3. Your friends vote you "Most Likely to Explode in a Fit of Rage."

4. Your sister tries to share the gospel message with you, not realizing you're already a Christian.

5. When you approach someone to talk about your faith, his first response is, "Please don't hurt me."

A Second Glance

The next time you find yourself in a crowd of people your age, pay attention to a couple of things. Where do your eyes drift? Who or what catches your attention? What are you thinking about other people as you look at them? What are you thinking about yourself?

Most guys are visual creatures. Whether we're checking out how good a girl looks or how well another guy is dressed, appearance is what gets our attention. We notice people who look or act a certain way. In other words, we respond to people in the *exact opposite* way God does.

The apostle Paul makes it clear in this verse that appearances of any kind—physical or otherwise—make no difference to him or to the God he serves. God cares only about a person's internal features. He can see the heart—so to him, everything else is just window dressing.

The fact that the majority of your peers tend to gravitate toward people who are good-looking or talented or popular or well dressed gives you a great ministry opportunity. Why not focus your attention on so-called average people? On guys who don't stand out in a crowd. On girls who don't turn heads when they walk past. On people who don't usually draw much attention.

Make an effort to treat these people as special. Get to know them. Let them know your interests go deeper than appearance. Show them you care more about who they are than about how they look. In other words, build some solid friendships based on substance, not style.

If you demonstrate an accepting spirit to others, you may find that they're likely to return the favor when you talk to them about your faith. Even better, they won't care how you look when you do it.

For more on accepting people who are difficult to accept, see Matthew 5:43-48.

 ## Appearances Can Be Deceiving

Think about the absolute worst day of your life in terms of your outward appearance. A day when your hair, your clothes, and everything else about you screamed, "Loser!" What if people had judged you then? They might have formed the opinion that...

- you gargle nuclear waste, based on the smell of your breath.

- you buy all your clothes pre-wrinkled.

- you coat your pillowcase with motor oil, based on your greasy hair.

- you've been colorblind since birth, based on your lack of clothing coordination.

- you grew three inches since putting on your pants in the morning, thus explaining why they look more like shorts.

Have Mercy!

Do to others as you would have them do to you.

Luke 6:31

This so-called Golden Rule would be a whole lot easier to obey if it read, "Do to others as they do to you," wouldn't it? That's the way things worked in Old Testament times. If a person caused you trouble, you were legally entitled to cause an equal amount of trouble in his life. The law was known as "an eye for an eye."

Jesus, however, calls his followers to a higher standard. No matter how much you might like to give someone a taste of his own medicine... or make someone pay for crossing you...or deal out revenge to an old nemesis, Jesus doesn't give you the option. Vengeance isn't part of his plan for your relationships—mercy is.

You know what mercy is, don't you? Mercy is undeserved favor. Mercy is what allows us to escape the punishment we deserve for the things we've done wrong. Mercy is what God shows us every day of our lives. If God is able to show us love despite the things we've done, how hypocritical is it for us not to do the same for others?

The first step in learning to live according to the Golden Rule is to take a big swallow of pride. Wounded pride is a traumatic injury for a lot of guys. It can cloud our judgment. It can make us lose sight of whom we serve and what God expects of us.

The next time you find yourself tempted to do to others as they do to you, think about the mercy God has shown you. Remind yourself that only he has the right to judge. Take comfort in the fact that his judgment is much more complete than anything you can come up with. And pray for God's help in swallowing your pride and responding in a way that pleases him.

For Jesus' instructions on how to treat enemies, check out Luke 6:27-36.

≫ Lesser-Known Rules

Everyone knows the Golden Rule: "Do to others as you would have them do to you." Here are some lesser-known rules—probably because living by them is a really bad idea:

The "You'll Get Yours" Rule

"Do to others as they deserve."

Be nice to nice people. Treat jerks like jerks.

The Supermarket Rule

"Do to others as a supermarket cashier does to you."

Give others exactly what they ask for—nothing more, nothing less.

The False Friend Rule

"Do to others as false friends do to you."

Be nice to others when you need them; treat them badly the rest of the time.

The Liar Liar Rule

"Do to others as politicians do to constituents."

Tell others how well you're going to treat them, then forget you made that promise.

The Fire Hydrant Rule

"Do to others as a dog does to a fire hydrant."

You really want an explanation?

Shocking Kindness

"Don't be afraid," David said to him, "for I will surely show you kindness for the sake of your father Jonathan. I will restore to you all the land that belonged to your grandfather Saul, and you will always eat at my table." Mephibosheth bowed down and said, "What is your servant, that you should notice a dead dog like me?"

2 Samuel 9:7-8

Mephibosheth was stunned that King David would show him kindness. Not because he pegged David as a bad guy, but because he knew how the world worked. God had taken the throne of Israel away from Mephibosheth's grandfather Saul. Saul was also now dead. So Mephibosheth had no political power in Israel. He was crippled in both feet, so he had no physical skills to offer David. His description of himself as a "dead dog" tells you all you need to know about Mephibosheth's self-image.

That's why it was such a shock to Mephibosheth when David reached out to him. He knew there was no hidden motive. David showed him kindness because he truly cared.

David's example is a great one for us to follow. Remember there's nothing special about being kind to people you like. There's nothing extraordinary about doing favors for people you want to impress or people who can do something for you in return. That's what many politicians do every day.

But being kind to people who have no reason to expect kindness from you and have nothing to give you in return? Now that's another thing altogether! In fact, that's the kind of thing that makes people ask, "What's up with that guy? What makes him different from everyone else who ignores me or makes my life miserable?"

The fact is, being kind to others will make you stand out—whether you like it or not. Many guys have a problem with showing kindness because they think it makes them look weak. In order to be kind, you have to drop your hard façade. You have to let people know you really care. You have to show emotion. You can't pretend to be jaded or uncaring. If you're willing to take that chance, you can bet God will use you to touch—and even change—people's lives.

For a more complete picture of the relationship between David and Mephibosheth, look at 2 Samuel 9:1-13.

 ## Ultimate Tests of Kindness

If you can show kindness to these people, you can show kindness to anybody.

1. The spammer who junks up your e-mail inbox.

2. Telemarketers who call during dinner.

3. The teacher with no social life who loads you up with homework over the weekend so that you can't have a social life, either.

4. The guy sitting in front of you at a football game who decides to stand for all four quarters.

5. Parents who say, "This hurts me more than it does you," before punishing you.

6. Siblings who smirk and make faces while your parents punish you.

7. The annoying actor on that TV commercial you hate.

8. The guy sitting next to you at a concert who sings and plays air guitar to every single song.

9. The guy your girlfriend likes more than you.

10. The person who stuck you with the nickname you despise.

What's Mine Is Yours

At mealtime Boaz said to her, "Come over here. Have some bread and dip it in the wine vinegar." When she sat down with the harvesters, he offered her some roasted grain. She ate all she wanted and had some left over.

Ruth 2:14

Ruth and her mother-in-law Naomi were in a desperate situation. Their husbands were dead. Their family was gone. They knew almost no one in Bethlehem. They had no one to look out for them. Fortunately for them, God brought a man named Boaz into their lives.

Boaz was a stand-up guy. For one thing, his heart was sensitive to people in need. He recognized that Ruth was in a desperate situation. And when he realized it, he didn't look away or leave it to someone else to help her. Instead he took the initiative to do something about it. It didn't cost him much up front, just some leftover grain from his field and a little water and bread. But that was enough to keep Ruth and her mother-in-law from going hungry. It was enough to save their lives.

Not only did Boaz help Ruth, he showed class while doing it. He didn't try to embarrass her or make her feel inadequate. He didn't say, "Here, you poor woman, I feel sorry for you, so I'm giving you this food." Instead Boaz treated her with respect. He helped her help herself. He allowed her to keep her dignity intact.

How can you follow Boaz's example? Do you know anyone in a desperate situation? Perhaps a homeless family in your area? Or a student who's new to your school and seems a little lost? Or a geeky guy with no friends to look out for him? Or an elderly neighbor who just lost a spouse?

If you're ready to make a Boaz-sized difference in the life of another person, ask God to give you the wisdom, patience, and generous spirit you need. You may be surprised by what God can do through you.

For the full story of Boaz's generosity to Ruth, check out Ruth 1:1-4:12.

 Questions You May Have about the Book of Ruth

1. Did Orpah, Naomi's other daughter-in-law, have her own daytime talk show?

2. Do you suppose people really called Naomi "Bitter" ("Mara"), like she asked them to (Ruth 1:20)?

3. Who would name a kid Boaz?

4. Did Boaz ever work part-time as a clown?

5. After what happened to her first husband and his family, do you suppose Ruth asked for a medical history from Boaz before she married him?

Show Some Respect!

*Rise in the presence of the aged, show respect for the elderly
and revere your God. I am the LORD.*

Leviticus 19:32

How do you feel about senior citizens? Be honest. Do you tolerate them for as long as you have to and then breathe a sigh of relief when you say goodbye? Do you avoid them as much as possible? Or do you show them respect and try to learn from them?

Many guys would probably roll their eyes at the last suggestion. The idea of learning something from some gray-haired people two generations past their prime seems ridiculous. After all, what could your grandparents possibly say to you that could make even the slightest difference in your life? What valuable lesson could your retired neighbor teach you that would even remotely relate to anything in your world? Why would you ever need to hear the wisdom of some elderly person in your church?

If you dismiss older people because they seem frail and feeble, or because everything they say seems out of date, not only are you disrespecting them but you're also cheating yourself out of a valuable life resource. If you take the time and effort to show elderly people respect—by listening to them, getting to know them, and asking them questions—you'll find out that they've seen, done, and learned things you can only dream about.

Keep in mind that the kind of respect God is talking about goes beyond being polite and using good manners. To "respect your elders" means taking an interest in what they have to say. It means honoring who they are. It means serving them. It means looking for ways to apply the lessons they've already learned to your own life.

In this entry's Bible verse notice how God connects respect for the elderly with reverence for him. The bottom line is you can't disrespect senior citizens and also have a healthy relationship with God. One is tied to the other. So take the challenge and start respecting.

For more on respecting the elderly, read through 1 Peter 5:5-11.

 ## Things You Might Say to Your Grandkids One Day

"When I was your age...." How many times have you rolled your eyes when you heard your grandparents start a sentence with those five words? Someday you may be using the same words with your grandkids—but the rest of your words may be very different:

- "When I was your age, vegetables didn't come in artificial flavors. Peas tasted like peas, cauliflower tasted like cauliflower, and beets tasted like...something you scraped off the bottom of your shoe."

- "When I was your age, cars didn't steer themselves. You had to turn a steering wheel."

- "When I was your age, we only had 500 cable channels to choose from."

- "When I was your age, people didn't wear disposable clothes. We had to wash our shirts and pants after we wore them."

- "When I was your age, we didn't have interactive worship technology. We had to go to an actual building every Sunday."

- "When I was your age, you couldn't access the Internet just by concentrating. You needed a computer."

- "When I was your age, I walked five miles to school every morning." (Every generation has to use that one.)

Your Honor

"Honor your father and mother"—which is the first commandment with a promise—"that it may go well with you and that you may enjoy long life on the earth."

Ephesians 6:2-3

The idea of honoring your father and mother goes beyond obeying them and even beyond showing them respect (although those two things are certainly a big part of it). Honoring your parents means treasuring them, being genuinely happy that they are part of your life, and telling them how you feel about them.

That's a tall order for many teenagers. The teen years are tough on the parent-child relationship. While teenagers are trying their hardest to become independent adults, parents are often reluctant to grant them independence. That leads to frequent conflict. And in the heat of battle, things like honor, respect, and family pride get tossed aside. The good news is no matter how bad things have been in the past with your parents, God will give you a second (and a third and a fourth…) chance to restore honor and pride to your relationship with them.

Are you proud of your parents? Have you ever given much thought as to who they are in the workplace…or in your church…or in your community? Have you ever talked to them about how much you appreciate the example they set for you? Beyond family pride, honoring your parents means caring for them and taking the time to make sure that their needs are being met instead of simply worrying about your own.

Think about the things you can do this week to honor your parents in a way that will make a difference in their lives. If your mom is overworked, why not volunteer to make dinner for the family one night? Or clean a bathroom? If your dad is on a tight schedule at work, why not make his life at home easier by washing the car, mowing the lawn, or shoveling snow?

In other words, instead of silently committing yourself to honoring your parents, demonstrate your honor in the way you live.

For more of God's instructions to families, check out Ephesians 5:22-6:4.

Odd Ways to Honor Your Parents

Some people prefer traditional parent-honoring methods. Some people prefer non-traditional methods. For the latter group, we present the following ideas:

1. You wear a temporary tattoo of their names...over each eyebrow.

2. You refuse their curfew of 11 p.m. and insist on being home every night by 8:30 p.m.

3. During your high school's next sporting event, you lead the crowd in a cheer for your dad.

4. You listen only to your mom's favorite radio station when you're in the car—even when she's not around.

5. You blow off the prom to stay home and play Monopoly with them.

6. You get rid of the clothes you wear now and create a whole new wardrobe for yourself—with the identical clothes your father has in his closet.

7. You keep a little shrine to your parents in your school locker.

8. You refuse to be someone's friend...unless they have the same name as your dad.

You Think You Know It All?

Moses listened to his father-in-law and did everything he said.

Exodus 18:24

Everyone in your life is a teacher...if you're willing to learn. Think about it. Each person you know has a unique set of life experiences. Each person in your neighborhood has a unique body of knowledge. Each person you pass on the street brings a distinctive perspective on the world. Each person on this planet has a one-of-a-kind set of opinions and creative ideas. Everybody brings something new and different to the table.

Think of it as God's gift to you. He's surrounded you with hundreds of potential teachers. He's given you the opportunity to pick their brains, to learn from their experiences and mistakes.

In order to take advantage of his gift, though, you have to swallow your pride and admit that you can learn things from even the most unlikely people. Like your elderly neighbor. Or your older sister. Or the weird exchange student at school. Or your youth leader. Or even, gulp, your parents.

Moses was the established leader of thousands of Israelites. People came to him for advice. Yet when his father-in-law spoke, Moses listened. And Moses was rewarded with some valuable advice—words of wisdom that ended up making him a better leader.

Learn from Moses' example. Treat every conversation as a learning opportunity. Make it your goal to come away with a little more knowledge and wisdom than you had before the conversation started. Even if it's just information about the person you're talking to, you're still feeding your brain. And you never know what facts may turn out to be useful someday.

Do yourself a favor: develop a curious spirit. Learn to ask appropriate questions at appropriate times. Instead of always thinking about what you're going to say next, think of what you can learn by listening. Take advantage of the gift God's given you.

To find out more about Moses' learning experience, read Exodus 18:13-26.

 ## Really Practical Knowledge

As you try to learn from the people around you, see if they can shed some light on what to do if you're ever faced with some of these situations:

1. How to respond when your girlfriend asks, "Do these pants make me look fat?"—and they do.

2. How to maintain your cool after you tell a joke that absolutely no one laughs at.

3. How to react when you meet your girlfriend's parents for the first time—and they tell you how much they love her old boyfriend.

4. What to do when you're a dinner guest at someone's house and, after your first bite, you realize your plate is piled high with the most disgusting dish you've ever tasted.

5. How to react politely when you see a guy with a really bad toupee or comb-over.

6. What to do when you realize at the end of the school day that your fly has been open since first period.

7. What to say when your aunt asks you if you *really* like the reindeer sweater she knitted you for Christmas.

8. How to look innocent when, after dozing off in church, you find everyone around you looking at you because you've been snoring.

SECTION 8

The Buddy System

Get Your Hands Dirty

Now that I, your Lord and Teacher, have washed your feet, you also should wash one another's feet. I have set an example that you should do as I have done for you.

John 13:14-15

Foot washing in Jesus' day was a disgusting job. The roads of that time were mostly dirt. The preferred footwear was the sandal. You can imagine how nasty people's feet got after a long day of walking. That's why lowly servants often were stuck with the job of foot washing. That's also why Jesus' willingness to take on the job himself was so astounding. Jesus showed his disciples that anyone who follows him has to be willing to do the jobs no one else wants to do. In New Testament times, that included foot washing. Today it could involve any number of tasks.

For example, who wants to reach out to the homeless people panhandling on the streets? Who wants to befriend the kid everyone else calls a freak? Who wants to respond with kindness to a bully who makes your life miserable? Who wants to donate money to support an orphan in Africa? Who wants to visit elderly people in a nursing home every month?

The temptation is to shun these opportunities to serve God. To think that we're above "getting our hands dirty" in the lives of other people. To think our personal schedule and agenda is more important than the work God has for us. In other words, the temptation is to leave that work for others to do. But we can't do that. Not after the example Jesus gave us.

If God himself could get down on his knees with a basin and a towel and wipe filth from the feet of the very people he created, it's

REVOLUTION DEVOTIONAL

tough to argue that we're above any task. So...are you ready to get your hands dirty and give up a little status in order to serve others?

In other words...are you ready to be like Jesus?

For the entire foot-washing story, see John 13:1-17.

 ## Jobs Worse Than Foot Washing

1. Cleaning the foot-washing cloths.

2. Donkey washing.

3. Massaging porcupines.

4. Carrying bad news to quick-tempered, evil kings.

5. Checking animal genders before allowing them on the ark (just ask Noah).

6. Israelite wrangling (just ask Moses).

Surrounded

I have heard many things like these; miserable comforters are you all!

Job 16:2

Have you ever tried playing one-on-five basketball? If you're a really good player, you might be able to compete for a few minutes. But before long, the grind of having to take on so many guys by yourself will wear you down. And eventually you'll cease to be competitive. And the game will lose its appeal. Basketball works best as a team sport. And so does life.

God doesn't intend for us to face the pressures...disappointments... expectations...tragedies...and uncertainties of life by ourselves. That's why he gave us fellowship. Bonding with other believers to create a support group through good times and bad. The question is will you take advantage of the opportunity he's given you?

Do yourself a favor. Find people to whom you can go for help when you really need it. When the bottom drops out of your world, you don't want to share your feelings with boneheaded friends who are just going to crack jokes or avoid the issue because they can't handle a deep conversation. You don't want friends who will point fingers for no good reason or offer cheap, simplistic answers to your problems. That's what Job's friends did, and they weren't much help.

Surround yourself with people who will empathize with you. People who will really listen to you. People who will make a genuine effort to comfort you.

Where do you find people like that? If you're serious about surrounding yourself with a support group of believers, God will make sure you hook up with the right people. You just need to keep your eyes and ears open at school, youth group, work, and any place else you go.

And make sure you're ready to offer to other people the same kind of support and encouragement that you're looking for. That's what a successful support group is all about.

For more information about getting involved with a group of believers, look through Ephesians 4:1-16.

 ## Rejected Mottos

Many support groups use mottos (such as "One day at a time") to identify what they stand for. Here are some you probably *shouldn't* use for your support group:

- Always ready to help...unless something else comes up.

- Stop bothering us with your problems.

- WWBD: What Would Batman Do?

- Miserable Comforters Are You All! (to quote Job 16:2)

- You Call *That* a Problem?

- Quality Tires Since 1926

- R.T.O.B.A.T.A.C.B.S.W.H.F.O.T.T.C.T.G.W.A.C.I.H.P.L. (i.e., Ready to Offer Biblical Advice to Any Christian Brother Struggling with His Faith or Trying to Come to Grips with a Crisis in His Personal Life)

Say What?

When Job's three friends, Eliphaz the Temanite, Bildad the Shuhite and Zophar the Naamathite, heard about all the troubles that had come upon him, they set out from their homes and met together by agreement to go and sympathize with him and comfort him. When they saw him from a distance, they could hardly recognize him; they began to weep aloud, and they tore their robes and sprinkled dust on their heads. Then they sat on the ground with him for seven days and seven nights. No one said a word to him, because they saw how great his suffering was.

Job 2:11-13

Job's friends cared so much about him that they gave up a week of their lives simply to sit with him. Saying nothing. Doing nothing. Sharing his grief. And letting him know they cared.

Imagine having friends like that. Better yet, imagine *being* a friend like that.

Believe it or not, you have the power to make a very real difference in a friend's life when he needs it most. You don't have to worry about saying the right thing. And you don't have to worry about making the proper gesture. All you need to do is listen.

If your friend is hurting, one of the best things you can do for him is give him a chance to talk about it. Encourage him to tell you what he's feeling inside...when he's ready. Be patient. Show him you're prepared to go the distance with him—as long as it takes. If and when he decides to talk, give him your full attention. Maintain eye contact with him. Help him see that you're truly interested in what he has to say.

Don't try to hijack the conversation with your own opinions. Don't try to solve his problems for him or tell him what you think he needs to do. Don't say dumb things like, "I know how you feel." Because you don't. All you know is how you *think* you would feel if you were in his situation. Avoid being judgmental. Don't jump on his case if he says things you don't agree with.

In fact, don't say anything for a while. Just listen. If he asks for your opinion, you can give it. Just make sure you do it in a loving, considerate way.

When he's finished, ask if you can pray with him about his situation. Turn the situation over to God. And let your friend know that you'll always have a listening ear to offer him.

For more on the importance of listening, read and think about James 1:19-21.

 ## Listening Checks

Want to know if someone's really listening to you? Try subtly injecting some of the following phrases into your conversations to see what kind of response you get:

1. "Before I became a guy..."

2. "Back on the mother ship..."

3. "When I was dating the Olsen Twins..."

4. "Eliphaz the Temanite..."

5. "...something my dad learned in the C.I.A."

6. "Testing, testing, one-two-three. Is this thing on?"

7. "Your fly's open."

SECTION 9

Lust & Sex

Get Out of There!

Flee the evil desires of youth, and pursue righteousness, faith, love and peace, along with those who call on the Lord out of a pure heart.

2 Timothy 2:22

Many passages in the Bible urge us to stand firm and fight the enemies of our faith—this is not one of those passages. This particular verse is talking about sexual temptation. And that presents a unique challenge—especially to teenage guys.

Look at the first word of the verse: *Flee.* Run away. Put as much distance as you can between yourself and sexual temptation. That's a pretty extreme solution. But it's a wise one. Because if you're a teenage guy, not giving in to sexual temptation is really difficult. That's not meant as an insult to you. It's just a fact of puberty. The problem is your hormones—those things you read about in sex ed classes. At your age, hormones exert a powerful influence.

What makes the situation especially tough is the fact that it doesn't take much to trigger a hormone surge. A glimpse of a half-naked girl in a magazine ad. A suggestive comment from a neighbor. A brief fantasy. Once lustful thoughts get started, they're nearly impossible to control.

That's why the best strategy for keeping both your actions and thoughts pure is to flee sexual temptation. Don't give lust a chance to get comfortable in your head. When you see something that you know could spark a hormone stampede, take action immediately. Change the channel. Turn off the computer. Walk away. Put as much distance as you can between you and the source of your temptation.

And pray. Ask God to help you reject your lustful thoughts and fill your mind with things that won't get you in trouble. You can also take the initiative in avoiding lust. Stay away from things you know can cause you problems—whether it's late-night TV, Internet surfing, or the magazine rack at your local convenience store.

To learn more about how to become a workman approved by God, read 2 Timothy 2:14-26.

 Fast Flee

How fast should you "flee the evil desires of youth"? As fast as...

- you go from 70 m.p.h. to 55 m.p.h. when you spot a police car in your rearview mirror.

- a rabid football fan leaves church on Sunday mornings during the NFL season.

- you change the TV channel when you're bored.

- you answer when your mom asks, "Who wants the last piece of pie?"

- you hit "Restart" on a video game when you screw up your first turn.

Don't Fight Alone

Daughters of Jerusalem, I charge you by the gazelles and by the does of the field: Do not arouse or awaken love until it so desires.

Song of Songs 3:5

In the verse above, Solomon uses poetic language to express his warning: "Do not arouse or awaken love." But you get the idea of what he's talking about, don't you? He's talking about guarding against letting your hormones run wild. Guarding against awakening desires that you just can't control—even when you think you can.

Guarding against lust. That's a tall order in our society. Especially when most TV commercials, billboard ads, music videos, and magazine covers seem designed to do the exact opposite. Producers and advertisers understand the power of sex appeal. And they will use it to get your attention every chance they get.

Avoiding the media's barrage of sexual temptations is difficult enough. But when you start dating—or just hanging out with girls— the struggle to keep lust in check gets even more intense. As you start to get comfortable with certain females, the tendency is to relax and let your guard down. And that's all the opportunity lust needs.

It usually starts innocently enough. But you know there's a point where innocent romance becomes not-so-innocent lust. You may call it first base, second base, or something else. Whatever the case, *that's* the point you have to stay away from. When lust gets even the tiniest foothold in your life, it sets in motion a pattern of sin that can do life-changing damage.

You *can* protect yourself from lust. But it won't be easy. We've already talked about the bad news—that is, the many people trying to stir up your lust for their own benefit. Now let's talk about the good news. In your corner you have one whose power far surpasses the power of the media—and the power of your hormones.

Prayer is your most effective weapon. If you'll ask God to help every time you feel tempted, he will. Whether it's 10 times a day or 100 times a day, God is ready to give you the strength you need to resist sexual temptation (check out 1 Corinthians 10:13). All you have to do is ask.

To learn more about the dangers of lust, check out Proverbs 5:1-14.

 ## Top-Seven Rejected Names for the Couple in Song of Songs

If you flip through the Song of Songs in your Bible, you'll notice the book is made up of a conversation between two people deeply in love. The names they chose for themselves are "Lover" and "Beloved." But perhaps they tried out other combinations before they settled on those. Here are some possibilities they may have rejected:

1. Apple Tree and Dove Eyes (Check out Songs of Songs 2:3 and 1:15.)

2. Snookums and Sweetums

3. King Dude and Shulammite Chick

4. keepnitreel and 2hot4u

5. Sleepless in Israel and Looking for King Right

6. Romy O and Julie 8

7. Pookie and Sweetie Pie

Worth the Wait

We rejoice and delight in you; we will praise your love more than wine.

Song of Songs 1:4b

When was the last time you heard a guy in the locker room bragging about how well he was able to keep his lust under control on a date? When was the last time you heard two guys arguing about which one of them was better at resisting sexual temptation with their girlfriends?

Purity isn't what you'd call a valuable commodity, as far as most guys are concerned. Thanks to the media and the society we live in, we're conditioned to believe that real men have sexual experiences—the more, the better. It not only takes guts, it also takes a serious determination to go against that way of thinking.

Let's face it: Sexual temptation is probably the toughest kind of temptation to resist. That's what makes the idea of saving sex for marriage so difficult. But since that's God's plan for his followers, that's the standard we need to set for ourselves. He designed us. He knows exactly what will bring us the most satisfaction and pleasure. All he asks of us is to follow his guidelines. The payoff will be tremendous. As long as we play by his rules.

Having sex outside of God's plan—meaning outside of marriage—is like secretly raiding the Christmas tree before Christmas morning. What joy is there if you open a gift that was intended for someone else? And even if the gift you opened early was meant for you, how would that make the gift-giver feel? Probably not very good.

When you have sex outside of marriage, you take and give a priceless gift at the wrong time and probably to the wrong person. And worst of all, it's certain that you are hurting the ultimate gift-giver, God, whose plan is for you and your future wife to enjoy sexual union.

To learn more about what the Bible says about sexual temptation, scope out 1 Thessalonians 4:3-8.

 Extreme Ways to Resist Sexual Temptation

- Lock yourself in a tiny, solitary-confinement cell.

- Have an iron blindfold permanently attached to your face.

- Vow to run away screaming every time you see a girl.

- Permanently attach yourself to your mom with a leash.

- Banish yourself to a small, uninhabited island.

- Permanently attach yourself to your grandma with a leash.

- Pay your friends to tackle you every time they catch you even looking at a girl.

- Wear a helmet camera every day that broadcasts everything you do.

- Ask your family to watch the video every night.

Constant Combat

Having put him to sleep on her lap, she called a man to shave off the seven braids of his hair, and so began to subdue him. And his strength left him.

Judges 16:19

This was the beginning of the end for Samson, the once-mighty warrior and judge of Israel. And he had no one to blame but himself. The big man was a victim of his own sexual desires.

Because Samson couldn't control his lust, he risked his life to sleep with a prostitute...hooked up with a woman who wanted him dead...walked into several traps laid by his enemies...revealed his most precious secret...lost his incredible strength...had his eyes gouged out...and ended up dying with the people he hated most.

The thing is most guys can identify with Samson. We know all too well how lust can mess up our thinking to the point where we're willing to sacrifice anything for some temporary gratification. What makes lust especially dangerous is that it never ends. We're constantly surrounded by sexual temptation. Our culture bombards us with sexual images 24-7. Internet pop-up ads. TV commercials. Music videos. Billboards. Not to mention the real-life girls we see every day.

With God's help, though, we can fight the battle against lust—and end up stronger than Samson in the process. The keys are to be constantly aware of what's going on in your brain and to take immediate action as soon as you start to feel tempted. If you give lust a second thought, you're in trouble. Because once the wheels of fantasy are set in motion, they're almost impossible to stop.

The moment you find yourself looking at a girl—or a picture of a girl—in a sexual way, you need to stop, admit to God what you're doing, and ask him to help you clear your mind. If you need to repeat that process 100 times a day, do it. God certainly won't mind. He's happy to help you as often as you need him.

For the sad story of Samson and Delilah's twisted affair, take a look at Judges 16:1-31.

 Signs That You're Going a Little Crazy for a Girl

1. You get her name tattooed on your arm...before you even talk to her for the first time.

2. You rent her favorite chick flicks...even when she's not around to watch them with you.

3. You change your hair color to match hers.

4. You don't mind singing karaoke duets with her.

5. You let her call you "Pookie Bear" in front of your friends.

6. You find yourself doing her homework—and her laundry—for her.

7. Her friends refer to you as "Pookie Bear."

8. Your friends refer to you as "Pookie Bear."

SECTION 10

Reaching Out

Time to Take Action

This is a trustworthy saying. And I want you to stress these things, so that those who have trusted in God may be careful to devote themselves to doing what is good. These things are excellent and profitable for everyone.

Titus 3:8

"Doing what is good" could include anything that helps another person or brings glory to God. That leaves room for a lot of possibilities. In 10 minutes, you probably could come up with a list of at least a dozen good things you could do this week.

Of course, coming up with ideas isn't the hard part. Putting them into practice is. Ask people why they don't make a habit of doing good for others, and you'll get all kinds of answers. Some will tell you they don't have the time. Others will tell you they feel awkward, not knowing how to approach someone in need. Still others may say they don't have the skills, experience, or wisdom to make a difference in another's life.

All of those are legitimate points. Doing good for others often involves a sacrifice of time and energy. Sometimes it results in some awkward conversations and situations. And sometimes it requires you to go beyond what you think you're capable of. But the rewards that come from knowing you've done something good for someone else far outweigh any inconveniences. Not to mention the satisfaction that comes from being part of God's will.

Why not give it a shot? To start, write down seven good things you can do in the next seven days to help your family...your friends...or people you don't even know. Your list might include baby-sitting a younger sibling so your parents can go out. Or helping a friend with math homework. Or raking leaves for an elderly couple down the street.

The possibilities are endless. So are the rewards. Not just for the people you help but for you. Learning to do good will change your life in ways you can't imagine.

For Paul's instructions regarding doing what is good, see Titus 3:1-11.

 ## Reducing Awkwardness

We mentioned earlier that doing something good for someone else sometimes results in awkward situations. Here are some tips for avoiding awkwardness:

1. After you've done something nice for someone, don't hold out your hand for a tip.

2. Don't talk about all the fun things you could be doing if you weren't stuck helping the person.

3. Before you ask, "May I help you across the street, ma'am?" make sure you're talking to a woman.

4. Don't continuously whistle the old Beatles' song "Help!" the whole time you're with the person.

5. Never use phrases like, "Oh, you poor pathetic creature."

6. When you're finished helping, resist the urge to say, "Now you owe me, big time."

No Yoke

Do not be yoked together with unbelievers. For what do righteousness and wickedness have in common? Or what fellowship can light have with darkness?

2 Corinthians 6:14

As a Christian, you walk a tightrope. On one hand, you have a responsibility to share your faith with people who don't know Jesus. In order to do that, you have to spend time with unbelievers. You have to build relationships with them if you want to be able to show them the love of Christ. On the other hand, you have a responsibility to remain pure—that is, obedient and faithful to God. In order to do that, you have to avoid being too heavily influenced by the ideas and behaviors of unbelievers. You have to make sure that your friendship with unbelievers doesn't cause you to compromise your relationship with God.

That requires you to be grounded in your faith. You have to know what the Bible says about how believers should act, and what they should stay away from. The more you know about God's Word and his plan, the less likely it is you'll be influenced in negative ways by your friends.

You also have to take a leadership role in your relationships with unbelievers. When situations arise where a dirty joke might be told...or the wrong kind of movie might be played...or an offensive song comes on the radio, you have to be proactive in making your standards clear. Instead of silently going with the flow out of fear of offending a friend, you have to speak up. A simple "I'm not into that kind of stuff" is usually effective.

Don't try to play the role of undercover Christian. Be open and honest about your faith and the life God has called you to. Unless your friend is seriously anti-Christian, he or she will learn to accept you. And maybe in time he or she will learn to accept Christ.

For more of Paul's warnings concerning getting too close to unbelievers, take a look at 2 Corinthians 6:14-7:1.

 ## Go Together Like...

An old song suggests that "love and marriage go together like a horse and carriage." What about the relationship between a believer and the sinful influence of the world? What images accurately convey the relationship between the two?

Believers and the sinful influence of the world go together like...

- Frosty the Snowman and a flamethrower.
- a freshly painted house and a three-year-old with dirty hands.
- a funeral and firecrackers.
- a huge zit and a date with the girl of your dreams.
- a canker sore and a mouthful of salt.
- toothpaste and chocolate.
- a thornbush and a balloon.
- a scratchy wool sweater and a sauna.

Common Ground

Then the high priest asked him, "Are these charges true?" To this [Stephen] replied: "Brothers and fathers, listen to me! The God of glory appeared to our father Abraham while he was still in Mesopotamia, before he lived in Haran."

Acts 7:1-2

Stephen was one of the earliest leaders of the Christian church. He'd been brought before the Sanhedrin—the Jewish leaders—to defend his Christian beliefs. And he was ready.

Stephen knew the secret to getting his point across was to find a way to capture people's attention. That's why he mentioned Abraham, and later, Joseph and Moses—three of the most beloved people in Jewish history. Stephen knew the religious leaders would listen to any argument based on Jewish history, so he used that in his talk about Jesus.

Learn from Stephen's example. Before you share your faith with someone, think about the things the person is really into—whether it's music, sports, video games, or something else. Use those interests as a springboard for talking about Jesus.

For example, let's say you have a friend who's a music freak. With a little computer research, you could find some lyrics or interview quotes from your friend's favorite bands about life...death...spirituality...priorities...or anything else interesting. You could then use those quotes to start a conversation about how the artist's perspective coincides or differs from the Bible's perspective. You could also burn a mix CD of some Christian songs (by artists similar to those your friend likes) and give it to him. Later you could ask him what he liked and didn't like about the music—and especially the lyrics.

Any common ground you can find will help your chances of being heard. Finding that common ground may take some effort on your part. But if the result is someone getting to know Christ a little better, isn't it worth it?

Take some time to think about friends and family members who don't have relationships with Christ. What interests or experiences can you use to build common ground?

To read Stephen's blistering words to the Jewish religious leaders, see Acts 7:1-8:1.

 Hard Words to Say

Stephen knew his audience didn't want to hear what he had to say. But he said it anyway. Here are some other situations that might require some fancy talking:

- Telling a busload of tired, hungry football players that your restaurant's all-you-can-eat buffet has closed early.

- Explaining to your ex-girlfriend's older (and bigger and meaner) brother why you broke up with her—and left her heartbroken and emotionally devastated.

- Doing a hilarious (and unflattering) impression of your science teacher, and then turning around to find her watching you.

- Staring blankly and intently into space as you try to recall answers for your English final, only to discover that you're looking directly at the test of the smart girl next to you—and that your teacher is watching you with a seriously displeased look in her eyes.

Be Ready!

Therefore go and make disciples of all nations, baptizing them in the name of the Father and of the Son and of the Holy Spirit, and teaching them to obey everything I have commanded you. And surely I am with you always, to the very end of the age.

Matthew 28:19-20

How comfortable do you feel talking about Jesus? If you're like most young Christians—and a lot of older ones, for that matter—you probably have some reservations about it. It's one thing to live *your* life for Christ. But when you start trying to introduce his truth into other people's lives, you're setting yourself up for rejection. Or worse.

Some believers are uncomfortable about sharing their faith because they're afraid they'll be asked questions they can't answer. Does that sound familiar to you? If so, keep in mind that it's not your job to prove Christianity true. Your job is to be open with people about what Jesus means to you, what he's done in your life, and what he has to offer. It's the Holy Spirit's job to help people recognize the truth when they hear it.

As with most things in life, the more you share your faith with others, the more comfortable you'll become doing it. And the more confidence you'll have when faith-sharing opportunities arise. The best way to practice sharing your faith is to start with friends, family members, and other people close to you. Once you get the hang of sharing the story of your own relationship with God...explaining key Bible passages...answering basic questions, you can gradually expand your scope. You can look for ways to talk about Jesus with people you don't know well.

Beyond that, the best thing you can do is stay constantly prepared to talk about spiritual things. You never know when an opportunity is going to present itself. So when it does, you've got to be ready to seize the moment.

If you have concerns or worries, talk to God about them. And then ask him to give you opportunities to share your faith. You'll be amazed at how he uses you.

For more information on Jesus' return to earth, check out Matthew 24.

 Six Ineffective Faith-Sharing Methods

1. Performing the entire book of Matthew...in mime.

2. Trying to concentrate hard enough to "teleport" the gospel into other peoples' minds.

3. Spamming people's e-mail accounts with ads that ask, "Who Wants to Learn about Jesus?"

4. Slipping Bible verses about hell into fortune cookies.

5. Bootlegging copies of *The Passion of the Christ* for your friends.

6. Approaching someone on the street and saying, "You look like a sinner, so you'd better listen to what I have to say."

Any Volunteers?

*Then I heard the voice of the LORD saying, "Whom shall I send? And
who will go for us?" And I said, "Here am I. Send me!"*

Isaiah 6:8

Here's a situation that may seem familiar to you: In class, your teacher
asks a question about something you forgot to study. Then she starts
looking around the room for someone to answer it. You slink down
in your seat, trying to make yourself invisible—praying that she won't
pick you. Ever had an experience like that?

Unfortunately, many believers react the same way when it comes
time to serve God. When they see a need or a service opportunity, they
do everything they can to make themselves invisible, hoping that God
will pick someone else to get involved.

And that's a mistake.

You see, Christian service isn't just about helping others. It's about
pleasing God and drawing closer to him. The best way to strengthen
your bond with your heavenly Father is through obedient acts of service. If you decline the opportunities he gives you to serve him, you're
the one who will lose in the long run.

The good news is that God gives second chances. Right now, he
may be looking for someone to explain forgiveness to a student at school
who's struggling with guilt. He may be looking for someone to start a
winter coat collection for the homeless people in your community. He
may be looking for someone to share his love by hanging out with the
guy at church who no one can stand.

Will you be that person? Will you step up to the plate like Isaiah did and say, "Here am I—send me"? Don't let excuses like busyness or inexperience stand in your way. Few people have enough free time to get involved in service projects. People who are serious about service *make* time. And most people who volunteer for service work have no idea what they're doing. However, they learn very quickly that when God calls someone, he also equips that person. He will not let a small matter such as lack of experience stand in the way of his work being done.

So what are you waiting for? It's time to volunteer!

Read more on Isaiah's assignment from God in Isaiah 6:1-13.

 Least-Popular Volunteer Positions

1. Javelin catcher

2. Patient for student dentists

3. Diaper changer at a daycare center

4. Bullet-proof vest tester

5. Hospital bedpan emptier

6. Human crash-test dummy

Helping the Underdogs

There will always be poor people in the land. Therefore I command you to be openhanded toward your brothers and toward the poor and needy in your land.

Deuteronomy 15:11

If there's one thing you need to know about God, it's that he has a soft spot in his heart for the underdog. The needy. Those who're often over-looked in our society.

What's more, God has a special place in his heart for people who side with the underdog. People who reach out to the needy. People who refuse to overlook the less fortunate.

We're not talking about simply having a social conscience. Or feeling sorry for people in need. Take another look at the verse for this entry. Notice the word *openhanded*? That's for people who argue that it's enough just to care about or pray for people in need. You see, be-ing openhanded requires personal interaction. It involves reaching out. Offering something of value—whether it's money, clothing, food, or time. Making a real difference in a person's life.

The good news is that anyone can do it. You don't have to be rich. You don't have to be outgoing. You don't have to live in a big city with homeless people or in a poor country. You can obey God's command to be openhanded to the needy regardless of your situation. Whether you realize it or not, you have something to give.

If you made up your mind to get involved in the life of someone in need, what could you do? Could you change the life of a younger kid (maybe even a sibling) in need of a mentor? Could you be an answer to prayer for a mentally challenged or wheelchair-bound student at your school? Could you supply enough money to buy a month's worth of food and medicine for an AIDS orphan in Africa?

The possibilities are endless! Look around, take the plunge, and find out how cool it is to help others.

For the scoop on God's commands concerning the needy, turn to Deuteronomy 15:1-11.

 ## Seven Really Bad Fundraising Ideas

1. All-you-can-eat tofu buffet.

2. Selling stained glass windows door-to-door.

3. "Guess the number of hydrogen molecules in this jar."

4. Bingo night at the church where all you do is sing "B-I-N-G-O" for three hours.

5. Cat wash.

6. Pre-autumn leaf collection, where you pull the leaves off trees in the summer so that homeowners won't have to rake them in the fall.

7. Specialized car wash only for blue 1993 Honda Accords.

SECTION 11

Self-Image

Why Not You?

Amos answered Amaziah, "I was neither a prophet nor a prophet's son, but I was a shepherd, and I also took care of sycamore–fig trees. But the LORD took me from tending the flock and said to me, 'Go, prophesy to my people Israel.'"

Amos 7:14-15

Amos lived a quiet, simple life as a shepherd and fig grower. And that's probably all he expected to be. But one day God changed his future when he called Amos to deliver one of the most important messages in Israel's history.

Seems like a strange assignment, doesn't it? After all, there were probably hundreds of better-qualified people in Israel to deliver the message. A religious scholar might have been a more obvious choice. Or a priest. Or perhaps even the king himself. But God doesn't always opt for the obvious choice, does he? He wanted Amos. Not because of anything Amos had done, but because Amos was his choice.

You can bet that more than once Amos wondered, *Why me?* But he didn't let his uncertainty or insecurity get in the way of his faithfulness. Amos just did everything God told him to do. And he let God take care of the results.

What job might God be calling you to? Being the point person for all the Christians at your school? Teaching a kids' Sunday school class? Organizing a fundraiser to benefit African kids orphaned by the AIDS pandemic?

What's your first reaction when you try to picture yourself in one of those positions? Do you consider yourself unqualified? Can you think of dozens of reasons why you shouldn't be called? Can you name dozens of other people who you think would do a better job? Such thoughts probably went through Amos's head, too. But he didn't let his initial doubts get in the way of doing what needed to be done.

Keep Amos' example in mind the next time you face a challenge or opportunity that intimidates you. Remember, it's not your power that's being tested—it's God's. He sees and knows your weakness, but nothing can stop his will from being done...through you.

For more of Amos' confrontation with Amaziah, check out Amos 7:10-17.

 ## Important Reminders for a Shepherd/Fig Grower-Turned-Prophet

- Sheep respond well to whacks on the rear with a staff. People usually don't.

- Squeezing a fig to determine its ripeness is okay. Squeezing a person to determine his or her spiritual maturity isn't.

- When you try to be humorous by saying something like, "Turn baa-aaa-ck to God," people don't appreciate it as much as sheep do.

- Lecturing crowds about how to prune a sycamore tree doesn't buy you a lot of credibility as a prophet.

Ego Check

Speak to him and say: "This is what the sovereign LORD says: 'I am against you, Pharaoh king of Egypt, you great monster lying among your streams. You say, "The Nile is mine; I made it for myself."'

Ezekiel 29:3

We've all seen them: football players who point to the sky after they score a touchdown. Or baseball players who bless themselves before they come to the plate. Do you think the athletes who make those gestures are sincerely trying to give glory to God?

Whatever the case, how quickly do *you* give glory to God for his work and his blessings? Are you ever tempted to claim some of that glory for yourself? Before you answer, consider God's words in the verse above.

They're directed to Pharaoh, the king of Egypt, who apparently tried to claim some awesome feats as his own. Pretty outrageous, right? After all, what kind of power trip would you have to be on to actually try to convince people that *you* created the Nile River? When you think about it, though, taking credit for the Nile really isn't much different from taking pride in the fact that you're good-looking. Or expecting praise because you were born with good hand-eye coordination, which gives you an advantage in certain sports. Or thinking you're something special because you're good with computers.

Remember, everything good comes from God. If you try to take credit for your talents and abilities, you're not much different from the egomaniac who ruled over Egypt thousands of years ago.

Keep in mind, too, that stealing God's glory can be done actively or passively. Trying to take credit for something God did is an obvious no-no. But failing to thank him or give him credit every chance you get is also a form of pilfering God's glory.

What steps can you take this week to make sure that God receives glory for the good things he's done in you?

For the full effect of God's prophecy against Egypt and its pharaoh, scope out Ezekiel 29:1-21.

 Extreme Methods to Keep Your Ego Intact

- Stand up at a school assembly, announce that you're having problems keeping your ego in check, and ask your fellow students to help make sure you stay humble.

- Wear a T-shirt with all of your deepest fears and insecurities listed on the front.

- Hire a classmate to make fun of you in public at least three times a day.

- Every night, just before you go to sleep, ask one of your parents or siblings to remind you of an embarrassing event from your past.

- Wear a nametag that reads, "I'm better than you" and let people respond to you in their own unique ways.

(In)Security Guard

The LORD said to him, "Who gave man his mouth? Who makes him deaf or mute? Who gives him sight or makes him blind? Is it not I, the LORD? Now go; I will help you speak and will teach you what to say."

Exodus 4:11-12

Look in a mirror. What do you see? A big nose? A zit? Someone who's a bit unsure of himself? Incompetent at times? We all feel that way every now and then.

But the person you see when you look in the mirror is nothing like the person God sees when he looks at you. You see weaknesses and shortcomings. God sees hidden strengths and surprising talents. You see the limitations of your power and ability. God sees the unlimited potential of *his* power and ability *in* you.

Take Moses, for example. Who knows what God saw in this guy? Moses had everything going for him, then he killed a man and became a fugitive. He was a dude who made a living leading farm animals back and forth across the desert. Serious self-esteem issues.

Yet God looked at Moses as he was herding sheep for his father-in-law and said, "There's the man I'm going to use to challenge one of the most powerful leaders in the world, rescue millions of people from slavery, and lead them across the desert to their new home." Moses didn't believe it, but God knew better. And, of course, God was right. Moses turned out to be the perfect man for the job.

What if Moses had allowed his insecurities to get the best of him? What if he'd refused to look beyond his shortcomings? What if he'd rejected the opportunity God gave him? Imagine all that he would have missed. And then ask yourself: *What does God see when he looks at me? What does he have in mind for me?*

God can and will help you look beyond your weaknesses and shortcomings to what he can do through you. Just ask.

For the account of Moses' encounter with God, check out Exodus 4:1-31.

 ## Other Excuses Moses Might Have Used

Moses tried to get out of God's assignment by claiming he was "slow of speech and tongue" (Exodus 4:10). When that didn't work, here are some other excuses he might have tried:

- "I had a bad experience in Egypt as a baby, and I really don't want to go back there."

- "I'm allergic to sand."

- "I get nervous in big crowds."

- "My Egyptian's a little rusty. No one will be able to understand me."

- "My sheep need me."

- "I don't have a pair of dress sandals to wear to Pharaoh's palace."

- "I have a terrible sense of direction. I get lost easily in the wilderness."

- "I only travel for business. Otherwise, I like to stay home with my family."

- "My wife doesn't know about my past in Egypt, and I'd like to keep it that way."

- "I think I feel a cold coming on (cough, cough)."

Life Beyond the Spotlight

Blessed are the meek, for they will inherit the earth.

Matthew 5:5

Jesus turned traditional priorities upside down in his Sermon on the Mount. In ancient times, people considered wealth and power to be signs of God's blessings. The meek were nobodies. Afterthoughts. People to be ruled over, stepped on, condescended to, or ignored by important people. And though we'd probably like to think of our society as being more tolerant than ancient Israel's, the fact is, things haven't changed all that much in the last 2,000 years.

Think about what it means to be meek in our culture. Who are the truly humble types? They're the guys who don't have to be first all the time. The guys who don't bask in the spotlight every chance they get. The guys who don't have a problem doing thankless jobs. The guys who don't need to get revenge. The guys who listen instead of trying to dominate conversations. The guys who realize they wouldn't have anything if it weren't for God. The guys who don't complain when things get tough—because they know God is in control. The guys who recognize all that God has done for them and give him all the credit instead of praising themselves.

Now think about the people who get ahead in this world. The go-getters. The self-promoters. The egomaniacs. The publicity hounds. The loud. The brash. The confrontational. The chest-thumpers.

In our culture we're so conditioned to reward superstars and celebrities that we often overlook the "little people" who make their success possible. Those are often the meek. And while it's tempting to want to be the guy in the spotlight, Jesus says the real rewards lie on the other side of fame. Talk about a great trade-off. If you're willing to forego temporary popularity, power, and notoriety in this world, you will have God's acclaim for eternity.

So what do you say? Are you ready to add some meekness and humility to your life?

To learn more about who Jesus singled out for blessing, check out Matthew 5:1-12.

 ## Beatitude Amendments

Jesus singles out eight groups of people for special blessings in the Beatitudes of Matthew 5:3-10. But what if he had expanded the list? Who else might he have included?

1. Blessed are the only children, for they will not have to give up closet space to a sibling.

2. Blessed are the good skiers, for they will know the thrill of double-diamond runs.

3. Blessed are the three-point shooters, for they will not get hacked driving to the basket.

4. Blessed are the geeks, for they will run the Internet.

5. Blessed are the Yankee fans, for they will celebrate many a World Series championship.

6. Blessed are the Chicago Cubs fans, for they will learn patience.

Get a Grip

Then Harbona, one of the eunuchs attending the king, said, "A gallows seventy-five feet high stands by Haman's house. He had it made for Mordecai, who spoke up to help the king." The king said, "Hang [Haman] on it!"

Esther 7:9

Do you know what led to such a tragic end for Haman? He thought somebody disrespected him. That's it. And he couldn't let it go. He obsessed over it. And he vowed to get even with Mordecai, the man who disrespected him.

Does that scenario sound familiar to you? Think about professional athletes who go off when they feel opponents disrespect them. For many guys, respect is more valuable than money.

Are you one of those guys? Have you ever lost your cool because you thought someone was disrespecting you? If so, you know the male ego is a fragile thing. When it's injured, it demands repayment—often in the form of revenge. "An eye for an eye" is how the Bible puts it. The problem is that revenge never satisfies. All it does is trigger your opponent's need for revenge. And a bitter cycle of hatred is created.

That kind of pride is a poisonous emotion. So are reactions such as jealousy and the lust for power. Those emotions create a cancer of the soul. Unless you cut them out, they will continue to spread, inflicting more and more damage until they ultimately destroy you. Just as they destroyed Haman.

If you're struggling with poisonous emotions, talk to God about them. Ask him to help you trace the roots of those feelings in your life. Ask him to help you deal with the experiences and attitudes that caused those emotions to take root. Ask him to help you calm yourself and get your head on straight so you won't do anything you'll regret later.

One of the ways God can actually help you is if you talk to someone about what's going on inside you. If you find that your emotions are too intense for you to control, don't be too proud to seek help from a trusted adult. You'll be glad you did.

For the full story of the devastating effects of Haman's pride, read through Esther 3:1-10:3.

 ## Temperature Raisers

Which of the following scenarios might cause you to unleash some poisonous emotions?

- The driver in front of you is doing 20 m.p.h. on a two-lane highway with a 40 m.p.h. speed limit. Oncoming traffic is too heavy for you to pass. His left turn signal's been on for three miles. He keeps hitting the brakes. He has a bumper sticker that reads, "Honk If You Love Jesus." So every time you hit the horn, he looks in his rear-view mirror, smiles, and waves.

- Your parents invite your new girlfriend and her family over for dinner. By the time you get home from practice, they're already at your house. As you walk in the door, you hear your mom talking about how she washes your sheets every morning because of how bad you smell.

- Your art teacher assigns you to create a model of your favorite food. Working day and night, you sculpt from clay an incredibly lifelike pepperoni, sausage, and mushroom pizza. Tubby, your family's beloved St. Bernard, mistakes it for a real pizza and devours it. You have to go to school the next morning and convince your teacher that your dog really did eat your homework.

- The guy who stole your girlfriend and took your starting position on the basketball team just got a promotion at the store you both work at. He's now your boss.

Who's Behind the Wheel?

But Naaman went away angry and said, "I thought that he would surely come out to me and stand and call on the name of the LORD his God, wave his hand over the spot and cure me of my leprosy."

2 Kings 5:11

Let's review Naaman's story. He was the commander of the Aramean (Syrian) army, which made him a very powerful man. But he also had leprosy, a skin disease that caused him tremendous pain and humiliation. Naaman had an Israelite servant who suggested that the prophet Elisha could cure Naaman's leprosy. So Naaman went to see Elisha. The prophet told him that if he washed himself seven times in the Jordan River, his leprosy would be cured.

And would you believe Naaman *got mad* at Elisha? Look at his words in the verse for this entry. Naaman wanted an instant cure. He didn't want to get dirty in the muddy Jordan River. He wasn't interested in obeying commands. He wanted a quick fix so he could get on with the things he wanted to do.

Pretty arrogant, right? But the fact is that Naaman wasn't much different from many people today who claim to follow God. Sure we talk a good game about wanting to obey God's will. But then we get so tied up in satisfying our own desires—hanging out with whoever we want, going wherever we want to go, doing whatever we think is fun—that we forget to humbly invite God to direct our steps.

Like Naaman, we expect God to bless us on our own terms. Maybe you've never let your arrogance show the way Naaman did. But when you take your life into your own hands...when you make important decisions without praying about them first...when you get involved with people who pull you away from your spiritual commitment, you're putting God in the back seat of your life. And that's no place for One who is all-powerful and all-knowing. Especially the One who can and will do amazing things with what you give him.

Find the full story of Naaman's bout with leprosy in 2 Kings 5:1-27.

 ## Seven Signs You Might Be Struggling with Arrogance

1. You demand that your younger siblings call you "sir."

2. When your dad asks when you're going to take out the trash, you tell him you'll have your people contact him.

3. You have your name stenciled across the back of your chair in homeroom class.

4. Your license plate reads "AROGNT1."

5. You autograph your classmates' yearbooks...before they ask you to.

6. In 2 Kings, you like Naaman better before he humbles himself and jumps in the Jordan.

7. You do a victory dance and high-five everyone around you every time you answer a question correctly in class.

Who Can God Use?

*Barak came by in pursuit of Sisera, and Jael went out to meet him. "Come,"
she said, "I will show you the man you're looking for." So he went in with
her, and there lay Sisera with the tent peg through his temple—dead.*

Judges 4:22

Have you ever wondered why God chooses the people he does to carry
out his work? Think about some of the unusual choices he's made. Jacob
was a guy who cheated his twin brother out of everything he had. David
arranged to have one of his best soldiers killed in order to cover up his
affair with the soldier's wife. Moses was guilty of murdering a man in
broad daylight. Paul had helped execute Christians for the Jewish leaders of his day. Yet God chose each of them to accomplish some incredible things.

Judges 4 tells the story of another unusual personnel choice by
God. Sisera was the commander of the enemy Canaanite army. After
the Israelites defeated the Canaanite troops, Sisera tried to escape.
Barak, the commander of the Israelite army, took off in hot pursuit,
determined to kill his adversary.

Sisera hid in the tent of a woman named Jael. What he didn't realize was that the man he was running from wasn't the person he needed
to fear. God chose not to give Barak the honor of killing Sisera. Instead,
he chose Jael for the task. While Sisera slept, Jael grabbed a tent peg and
a hammer, snuck into the tent and, well, let's just say she gave Sisera a
splitting headache.

In the male-dominated culture of that time, God's decision to use
Jael for such a task was pretty amazing. But that's what makes following

God such an adventure. You never know what he might choose to use you for.

No matter what your past is...no matter what other people say about you...no matter how ill-equipped or unprepared you feel, God can do something incredible with you. Whether you can imagine it or not. What you need to do is maintain a willing spirit, listen for his call, and let God work.

Read about Sisera's gruesome death at the hands of Jael in Judges 4:1-24.

 Sisera's Last Words?

The Bible doesn't tell us what Sisera said before he died. Here are six possibilities:

1. "Why should I worry about Jael? She's just a woman. What could she do to me?"

2. "Will you please stop that pounding? I've got a splitting head-ache."

3. "I'll say this about Jael: She really knows how to drive her point home."

4. "Peg? Who's Peg?"

5. "Will somebody please help me up? I think my head's caught on something."

6. "Ouch."

Credit Where Credit Is Due

Now Moses was a very humble man, more humble than anyone else on the face of the earth.

Numbers 12:3

The next time you watch ESPN, try counting the number of ego displays you see. You know the kind of look-at-me celebrations we're talking about: a basketball player pounding his chest after a dunk, a lineman stomping around after a sack, a baseball player flipping his bat away after a home run.

If you're like most guys, you've probably done your share of posing and celebrating in pickup games with your friends. It's human nature, right? (Or maybe it's just a guy thing. Whatever.)

The problem comes when you really start to believe your own press. Especially when it comes to spiritual things. If you live the kind of life Jesus calls his followers to, people are going to notice. What's more, God may choose to use you in some high-profile way—maybe even as a leader.

If and when that happens, you're going to have to decide how you will handle the attention and acclaim that come your way. The best thing you can do in that situation is look to Moses as a role model. Moses wasn't the type of guy to strike a pose after doing something good. So it might be tempting to assume he had a weak self-image. The truth is that Moses' humility demonstrated great confidence in God. Moses knew exactly who and what he was—a faithful guy being used by God to do some incredible stuff. He also knew exactly who deserved the praise and attention for the things he did—God. Maybe that's why God used him in such remarkable ways.

If you learn to be humble about your talents and abilities, giving all the credit to the One who made you, God will use you to do incredible things, too, as he did with the unassuming Moses.

For more on humility, check out Philippians 2:1-11.

 Eight Lessons in Humility

Here are eight situations that could humble even the proudest guy:

1. Striking out in a slow-pitch softball game.

2. Drawing a blank when an attractive girl asks for your telephone number.

3. Singing (in a very loud voice) the wrong words to a song in church.

4. Walking into a sliding glass patio door at your girlfriend's house.

5. Being mistaken for a girl at a Halloween party...when you're not wearing a costume.

6. Missing an easy foul-ball catch at a baseball game...while a TV camera captures every moment.

7. Having that foul ball hit you on the head...with the TV camera still rolling.

8. Seeing clips of the incident later that night on TV.

SECTION 11: SELF-IMAGE

SECTION 12

Character

Thought Control

*Finally, brothers, whatever is true, whatever is noble, whatever is right,
whatever is pure, whatever is lovely, whatever is admirable—if anything
is excellent or praiseworthy—think about such things.*

Philippians 4:8

Your assignment is simple: Do not think about pizza. Got that?
Whatever you do, don't imagine yourself cutting a slice and trying
to catch the gooey cheese as it oozes over the sides. Banish from your
mind all thoughts of pepperoni, mushrooms, green peppers, tomato
sauce, and crust. Think about anything else in the world except pizza.
Ready? Go.

How well did you do? Are you suddenly hungry for pizza?

Controlling the mind is extremely difficult. The brain is like the
wild card of the body. If you want to stop your leg temporarily from
moving, you can do it. If you want to stop your eyes temporarily from
seeing, you can do that, too. With the cooperation of the brain. If, however, it's your brain that you want to control, you'll find it's not nearly
as cooperative.

That's why the apostle Paul's instructions in the verse above are so
challenging for believers. Paul understood that bad thoughts (whether
they involve lust, jealousy, violence, or something else) are like infec-
tions in our minds. Unless we get rid of them, they begin to spread.
But instead of listing things not to think about, Paul offers another
approach for dealing with bad thoughts. You see, the best way to keep
bad thoughts from spreading is to fill our minds with good thoughts
and not allowing bad thoughts room to move.

If you can't stop thinking about, say, a dirty joke you heard on the radio while driving to school, try thinking about the lyrics to a song with a solid message. Or your favorite Bible verse. Or a list of things to praise God for.

In other words, keep your mind occupied with good stuff. Don't give it a chance to dwell on things it shouldn't.

For more of Paul's instructions to Christ's followers, read over Philippians 4:1-9.

 **Mind Fillers**

Can't think of anything to fill your mind in order to keep bad thoughts out? Try these:

1. The Greek alphabet.

2. The active and inactive ingredients of Drixoral, Sudafed, and Benadryl.

3. The travelogue of the Israelites in the wilderness, according to Numbers 33.

4. The fine print on your parents' mortgage papers.

5. The recipe for your favorite chocolate chip cookies.

6. The legal disclaimer at the end of a car commercial.

7. The list of the new residents of Jerusalem in Nehemiah 11.

Pulling Your Weight

Now you are the body of Christ, and each one of you is a part of it.

1 Corinthians 12:27

If you know someone with a disability—an arm or leg that doesn't work properly, an impaired sense of sight or hearing—chances are that you've noticed how remarkable the body is able to compensate for its shortcomings. Most disabled people refuse to let their disabilities keep them from doing what they want to do.

All things being equal, though, most people would agree that nothing can replace a body in which all parts function properly. That goes not just for the human body, but the body of Christ as well—the church.

The body of Christ isn't a volunteer organization. If you're a Christian, you can't choose whether or not you want to participate in it. You're automatically a part of the body the moment you trust Jesus as your Lord and Savior. The questions you have to ask yourself are: Are you a productive part of the body or are you a disabled limb? Are you carrying your weight or are you making others carry you? Are you putting your skills to use in your church or are you just sitting back and watching other people do all the work?

Sitting back and watching is tempting. Especially when you're surrounded by people who seem more mature, more eager, and more qualified to do God's work than you. Remember, though, each part of the body has a different purpose. Some members of Christ's body may be able to do things you can't. But by the same token, you may be able to do things that other "body parts" can't. Every part is necessary. And if one part isn't functioning properly, the entire body suffers. That's why it's important for you to find your place in the body of Christ. We're all depending on you.

Find out how the body of Christ works from 1 Corinthians 12:12-31.

 **Body Image**

Sure, everyone wants to be the arms, legs, hands, and feet of the body of Christ. But what about the less-popular body parts? The next time you're in church, look around at your fellow worshippers—your fellow members of the body of Christ. Try to figure out who might be...

- the epiglottis.

- an eyelash.

- a toenail.

- an earlobe.

- the small intestine.

- the stirrup (the tiniest bone in the body).

- the femur (the largest bone in the body).

- the right ventricle.

- a gum.

- a knee cap.

- the esophagus.

- a nose hair.

What's Your Problem?

*I do not understand what I do. For what I want to do
I do not do, but what I hate I do.*

Romans 7:15

The words in this entry's verse sound like they come from a typical guy, don't they? From a regular fellow being pelted on all sides by temptation. An average Joe whose sinful nature is always threatening to bust out in a big way. A guy who knows firsthand what kind of damage that problem sins can cause.

If you know anything about the book of Romans, you know that those words in this entry's verse come from the apostle Paul himself. Think about that! This was a guy chosen by God to help start the first churches, to spread the word about Jesus to people who knew nothing about him. This was the guy who wrote more books of the Bible than anyone else, for crying out loud!

Yet he wrestled with the same feelings of guilt, self-loathing, and helplessness the rest of us wrestle with. If a guy like Paul struggled with those things, it's probably safe to say that no guy is immune to them. Don't misunderstand Paul's words, though. Yes, sometimes he became frustrated by the power of the sins that tempted him, but he wasn't a quitter. He refused to give up the fight. Every time his sin knocked him down, he got back up for another round.

That's the secret to dealing with problem sins: a fighting spirit. No matter how long you've been doing something...no matter how strong a temptation is in your life...no matter how impossible-to-give-up a habit seems, you have to fight. So put on your game face. Shift into warrior mode. Stop treating your problem sin like a comforting friend and start treating it like the enemy it is.

In other words, with God's help, prepare yourself to go the distance in your fight

To learn more about how to fight the battle against sin, check out Romans 7:7-25.

 ## Less-Than-Effective Attitudes in Fighting Problem Sins

- "It just seems so negative to say, 'No, no, no' to temptation all the time."

- "Fighting never solved anything. I prefer to reason with my temptation."

- "It could be worse. Just be thankful my problem sin isn't murder."

- "You don't understand. This is my signature sin. It's what people know me for. If I give it up, I'll lose my identity."

- "I'm a lover, not a fighter—especially when it comes to temptation."

Talent Show

Another of his disciples, Andrew, Simon Peter's brother, spoke up, "Here is a boy with five small barley loaves and two small fish, but how far will they go among so many?"

John 6:8-9

As you read about this miraculous chow-down for 5,000, your first likely response is amazement at Jesus' power and compassion for people. But there's another lesson buried in this story that we need to be aware of.

Think about the food Jesus used to feed the crowd. The five loaves and two fish. Where did they come from? From a boy in the crowd. Surely the kid had no illusions about his meager meal making a dent in the crowd's hunger. But he was willing to share what he had, for whatever it was worth. And he soon found out just how much his contribution *was* worth.

The lesson for us is never to underestimate God's ability to use even the smallest, most seemingly insignificant things we bring to the table. The fact that the kid in this story had only five loaves and two fish didn't bother Jesus. He didn't say, "I've got 5,000 people to take care of, and this is the best you can do?" Instead, Jesus took the boy's gifts, blessed them, and used them to feed the entire crowd (with food to spare).

Don't get fooled into thinking that you have nothing to offer God or the people around you. You do—because God has given you everything you need to carry out his work. What's more, he's ready to multiply your efforts into something amazing—just as he did the boy's meal. Remember, success doesn't depend on what you've got, but on

Jesus' awesome power to use what you've got. So give him everything you have and say, "Here, Jesus. It isn't much, but you can have it all."

And then prepare yourself for something amazing.

For the whole story of the miraculous feast, read John 6:1-15.

 Unanswered Questions

The story of Jesus feeding 5,000 people with five small loaves and two fish leaves some questions unanswered. For example...

- Did the disciples receive tips for serving the people?

- Did the kid get served first?

- What about condiments?

- Why was the kid walking around with two fish?

- Without a cooler, how did he keep the fish fresh?

- How much of the leftovers did the kid get?

- What did the kid say when his parents asked him what happened to his loaves and fish?

- How many dinner invitations did Jesus get afterward?

- What did the vegans in the crowd eat?

Whaddaya Got?

From everyone who has been given much, much will be demanded; and from the one who has been entrusted with much, much more will be asked.

Luke 12:48b

Do you think you've been given a lot? Not by your parents...or your grandparents...or an especially generous girlfriend...but by God. How much has he blessed you with? In taking stock of your personal inventory, don't just think in terms of money and possessions. Think also about your natural skills, your physical health, your family situation, your friends, and the opportunities you've been given. The whole package.

When you take all that into account, where do you stand? Before you answer, carefully consider your measuring stick. Compared to the wealthiest people you know—the guys who drive their own convertibles to school or spend summers in Europe—you may not come off well. However, compared to most of the world's population, chances are, you're off the charts.

Now here comes the million-dollar question: Based on what you've been given, what does God expect of you? Remember, he's given you what you have for a reason. He has a grand plan for making a difference in the world through you. Are you on board for it? Are you ready to accept the responsibilities that come with God's generosity?

Think about it. What steps can you take to live up to God's expectations for your life? Be specific. For example, what can you do with your spending money that will make a difference in a needy person's life? How can you use the healthy body God's given you to assist less-fortunate people? Who can you invite into your circle of friends and offer the kind of camaraderie and fellowship you've been blessed with? What unique service opportunities can you contribute to?

Those are the questions you need to ask yourself now. Because one day God will ask you what you did with what he gave you. And you'll want to have a good answer for him.

For Jesus' comments concerning being faithful and wise servants, check out Luke 12:35-48.

 ## From Everyone Who...

"From everyone who has been given much, much will be demanded." That's one rule of thumb for living. Here are some other (non-biblical) ones:

- From everyone who has been given packs of gum, many pieces will be demanded.

- From everyone who has been given tubs of popcorn at the movies, many handfuls will be demanded.

- From everyone who has been given the answers to tests, much information will be demanded.

- From everyone who has been given bad breath, much distance will be demanded.

- From everyone who has been given cars, many rides will be demanded.

- From everyone who has been given the ability to do card tricks, many demonstrations will be demanded.

- From everyone who has been given reprimands at practice, many laps will be demanded.

Wise Guy

*For the L**ORD** gives wisdom, and from his mouth come knowledge and understanding.*

Proverbs 2:6

Here's the scenario. Your eccentric elderly neighbor died recently, leaving behind no living relatives or heirs. Word gets out that before he died, he hid a small fortune somewhere in your immediate area. How would you respond if you knew there was a large stash of money in a nearby secret location, just waiting to be found? Probably run pretty quick to start looking.

What if you discovered there was something far more valuable than money—namely, wisdom—hidden in a not-so-secret location, just waiting to be found by some lucky person? Would you pursue it as hard as you'd pursue money? If not, you should.

As treasure hunts go, the search for wisdom probably seems a lot less exciting than, say, a search for a million dollars. But can money help you when you're struggling with doubts about God or about how to live your life? Can money give you clear direction when you're not sure about your future? Can money help you resist a temptation that could potentially destroy your life?

Wisdom can do all those things and more. Wisdom can bring you closer to God. Wisdom can change the way you look at the world. And wisdom can change your role in the body of Christ.

If you'll commit yourself to gaining wisdom, people will notice changes in you. They'll begin to see you as a mature believer. They may start to come to you for answers and advice. In time, you may even find yourself mentoring other believers. Imagine being able to make a difference in someone else's life! That's what wisdom can do for you.

Are you ready to start searching for it? The map is your Bible, and the starting place is the book of Proverbs. The search won't be easy. And it won't be short. In fact, it will last the rest of your life. But the rewards will be more than worth the effort.

For the long list of wisdom's benefits, take a look at Proverbs 2:1-4:27.

 ## Signs That You May Need to Seek Wisdom a Little Harder

1. You're still thinking about that dead neighbor's hidden loot from the opening illustration of the devotion.

2. The idea of opening your Bible to the book of Proverbs makes you feel tired all over.

3. Your idea of making a long-term investment is buying clothes for next season.

4. You made your own mental list of things money *can* do that wisdom can't.

5. You think your good grades mean you already have wisdom.

Mr. Clean

At this, the administrators and the satraps tried to find grounds for charges against Daniel in his conduct of government affairs, but they were unable to do so. They could find no corruption in him, because he was trustworthy and neither corrupt nor negligent. Finally these men said, "We will never find any basis for charges against this man Daniel unless it has something to do with the law of his God."

Daniel 6:4-5

The Babylonian officials were like tabloid reporters. They were desperate to dig up any dirt they could find on Daniel. Except that Daniel gave them very little to work with. So, like most tabloid reporters, the officials had to create their own dirt.

It's human nature to look for flaws, weaknesses, and scandals in other's lives. And let's be real here—usually you don't have to look very hard to find those things. After all, no one's perfect, right? But what if someone couldn't dig up any dirt on you? If you had a spotless record like Daniel's, what kind of message would it send to those who know you? What would it say about God's work in your life?

Unless you've just moved to a new area where no one knows you, chances are excellent that the people closest to you are well aware of many of your mistakes and failures. And there's nothing you can do to change that.

But you can do something about today. And tomorrow. And every day after that. Starting right now, you can live your life with the same kind of intense devotion to God that Daniel had. Are you ready to start?

To find out how the Babylonian officials set up Daniel and got him sentenced to death, read Daniel 6:1-28.

 Any Accusation Will Do

The Babylonian officials were looking for any excuse to get Daniel in trouble. If they'd gotten really desperate, they might have used some of these:

- The nameplate on his office door reads "Daniel" (his Hebrew name) instead of "Belteshazzar" (his Babylonian name).

- He's a vegetarian. The royal chefs hate him.

- He's a friend of those fiery furnace freaks.

- He sees weird visions.

- He talks with an accent.

- He's a dreamer.

- Sometimes he has "bed head" in the morning.

Take the Lead

Day after day men came to help David, until he had a great army, like the army of God.

1 Chronicles 12:22

Do you consider yourself a leader? Many guys probably would answer no to that question. They prefer to remain safely anonymous followers rather than sticking their necks out and drawing attention to themselves by trying to take charge.

What David discovered, though, is that you can become a leader without really *trying* to take charge or make changes happen. If you commit yourself to following God, others will notice and want to join you—maybe even follow your example. Leadership has very little to do with titles or chains of command. Leadership is about influence. It's about getting people to do the right things.

You've heard about peer pressure your entire life—how there's no avoiding it, how it corrupts good kids, and how it's the ultimate persuader. But what if *you* are the one exerting the pressure? What might happen if instead of being influenced to party as often as possible...pick on the weak...and blow off anything that seems too spiritual, your friends and classmates felt peer pressure from you to find God-honoring ways to have fun...help people in need...and talk about what they believe? *That's* the kind of influence a leader can have.

Do you have what it takes to be a leader? The answer is yes. You do have what it takes. You have God's Holy Spirit in you. And that's all you need. The question is, are you going to take advantage of your leadership opportunities? Remember, you don't have to be president of your class or youth group to be a leader. You can be a leader among your group of friends or in your neighborhood or at your job. All it takes is the confidence and desire to do what you know is right and encourage others to do the same.

For the full story of how David became a leader of warriors without really trying, check out 1 Chronicles 12:1-40.

 Five Things Almost Every Leader Hears

1. "I didn't vote for you, so stop telling me what to do."

2. "Who died and left you in charge?"

3. "Who's going to make me?"—usually spoken by a guy much larger than the leader.

4. "You've really turned into a jerk"—usually spoken by a leader's friend who doesn't like one of the leader's decisions.

5. "You're not the boss of me"—usually spoken by a younger sibling.

Beyond Sorry

After I strayed, I repented; after I came to understand, I beat my breast.
I was ashamed and humiliated because I bore the disgrace of my youth.

Jeremiah 31:19

Have you ever *really* disappointed someone? Have you ever done anything that made people change their opinion of you—for the worse? Maybe it involved getting caught going too far with your girlfriend. Maybe it had to do with some embarrassing files on your computer hard drive. Or maybe it occurred when you came home wasted after a party.

If you've ever had such an experience, you know what regret feels like. You know what it's like to want to go back and erase what you did. To want to stop people from being disappointed in you.

That's what genuine repentance is like. It's the desire to get rid of your sin and start over so that God will look at you with pride again.

Too often repentance gets overlooked in our communication with God. When we feel guilty about something we've done, the usual pattern is to offer up a quick prayer of apology, ask God for forgiveness, and then get on with our lives. Occasionally we remind ourselves of a verse like 1 John 1:9 ("If we confess our sins, he is faithful and just and will forgive us our sins and purify us from all unrighteousness")—just for extra assurance. And in the process, we skip over repentance.

You see, sometimes it's not enough simply to say, "I'm sorry," after letting someone down—especially when that someone is God. Sometimes we need to give ourselves time to experience regret over our actions in order to fully appreciate God's forgiveness.

One of the best ways to generate true feelings of repentance is to spend some time thinking about what Jesus did on the cross. Thinking about his love for you. Thinking about who he is. The more we know and understand who it is we have sinned against, the more we will experience genuine, heartfelt repentance for our sins. Ask God to show you who he is. Ask him to help you repent. That's a prayer he will never refuse!

To learn more about repentance, check out 2 Corinthians 7:8-13.

 ## Bad Ways to Convince a Friend to Repent

- Throw a brick with REPENT written on it through his bedroom window.

- Tattoo a large "R" on his hand.

- Whenever he tries to talk to you, say nothing but "repent" over and over again.

- Brand a large "R" on his forehead.

- Call him every night at 2 a.m. and say "repent" over and over again.

- Shave "Repent" into the top of his head.

- Get all his friends to surround him and chant "Repent! Repent! Repent!"

Above and Beyond

He overlaid the inside with pure gold. He paneled the main hall with pine and covered it with fine gold and decorated it with palm tree and chain designs. He adorned the temple with precious stones. And the gold he used was gold of Parvaim. He overlaid the ceiling beams, doorframes, walls and doors of the temple with gold, and he carved cherubim on the walls.

2 Chronicles 3:4b-7

The Bible doesn't tell us how much money Solomon spent to build God's temple. But the description of the construction and the furnishings goes on for pages. The bottom line is that everything was made of the finest materials and covered with gold. It's safe to say that money was no object for the king of Israel.

But apparently "good enough" wasn't good enough for Solomon. He could have lowered his sights a little, cut a few corners to save time and money, and still created an impressive temple for God. But Solomon viewed his work on the temple as a gift to God. And he wasn't about to offer anything less than his best to God. That's why Solomon sweated every detail and spared no expense to create something truly spectacular.

Do you bring that same attitude to God's table? Chances are you'll never be asked to build a worship center for God. But that doesn't mean you won't be given a similar opportunity: a chance to use what you have to do something useful for God. When the time comes, will you throw yourself into the task with the kind of fervor that Solomon demonstrated? Will you refuse to cut corners? Will you sweat the details? Will you strive for something truly spectacular?

Not for your sake or your glory…but for God's glory?

Think about what you have to offer. Is it a talent for art or music? An ability to build or fix things? A knack for organizing or managing a project? Think about why God has given you your particular set of skills and abilities. Think about how you can present your gifts to God in a way that goes beyond just "good enough" and becomes spectacular.

To see all the ways Solomon made excellence his goal, take a look at 2 Chronicles 3:1-7:22.

 Signs That You Probably Haven't Achieved Excellence

- Your teacher doesn't draw a smiley face on your research paper before she hands it back.

- You sleep 16 hours a night.

- You spend more time playing video games than you do anything else...including sleep.

- After you finish your class presentation, the only response you get from your classmates is a single "Huh?"

- Your coach benches you...30 seconds after sending you into the game.

- You get a D- on an important test, and your mom posts it on the refrigerator.

SECTION 12: CHARACTER

Reapin' the Rewards of Motivation

How long will you lie there, you sluggard? When will you get up from your sleep?

Proverbs 6:9

If you have a hard time rolling out of bed in the morning, the verse for this entry may sound a little too familiar to you. Like maybe something your mom or dad yells in frustration when they're trying to wake you up. If that's the case with you, you can relax. We're not going to pile on. Your sleeping habits are between you and your parents.

What's more, this passage isn't just about laziness; it's about opportunity.

Every day carries with it the opportunity to learn something new—perhaps even something life-changing. Every day brings a new opportunity to start an important relationship—with someone who may turn out to be a friend, a mentor or...something even better. Every day offers the opportunity to accomplish something meaningful—if not for you, then for someone else. Every day gives you a new chance to influence people's impression of you. The question is, are you ready to take advantage of the opportunities that come your way?

The key is self-motivation. Generating the energy and determination to grab every day that God gives you and squeeze every bit of potential out of it that you can. Do you have that kind of self-motivation? If your mom or dad gives you an instruction—such as, "Clean the garage before you go to your friend's house"—and then leaves you alone to finish the job, what are the odds you'll actually get it done?

People respond to self-motivation in others in big ways. If you get a rep as Mr. Dependable—someone who doesn't need to be baby-sat or nagged, someone who enjoys tackling the challenges that each new day brings—you'll find that extra freedom, extra independence, and extra privileges come with it.

And that's just the beginning of God's rewards for people who refuse to be sluggards.

For more warnings against wasting time, check out Proverbs 6:1-19.

 ## Signs That You May Need Some Spiritual Motivation

1. You get lost driving to church because you can't remember how to get there.

2. You get hung up in a prayer because you can't remember what comes after "In Jesus' name."

3. You can't find the book of Genesis in your Bible.

4. You refer to your youth leader as "What's-his-name."

5. You choose to watch a rerun of Game 3 of the 1984 National League playoffs on *ESPN Classic* instead of going to Bible study.

6. The pages of your Bible crumble to dust when you open them.

7. You start to believe your spiritual gift is the ability to sleep through any sermon.

Get Out of the Mud

The priests and Levites had purified themselves and were all ceremonially clean. The Levites slaughtered the Passover lamb for all the exiles, for their brothers the priests and for themselves.

Ezra 6:20

Think about the last time you tried to clean yourself up after getting really, *really* dirty. Like, say, after a "mud bowl" football game. Or after painting a house. Or after laying tar on a driveway. Think about how the dirt and grime seemed to cling to you like a second skin.

That's what sin is like. It mucks up our insides. It clings to us like a stench. Worst of all, though, it interferes with our relationship with God. Here's why: God is holy. That means he is pure, completely removed from sin. Sin cannot exist in his presence. So in order for us to be his people, we too have to be pure.

Of course, none of us can purify ourselves. We need Christ to do that for us. Jesus' death on the cross paid the eternal cost for our sins. It justified us and made us pure in God's eyes. But it didn't eliminate our sinful urges. And it didn't erase the personal consequences of our sinful actions. Sin creates a disturbance in our intimacy with God. One with sin in his life that he hasn't confessed and for which he hasn't asked forgiveness will feel distant from God. That's part of his design for us.

In the Bible there's a tight relationship between purity and obedience. Obedience involves a heart that's right before God. You may be able to fool other people with a fake purity act, but you won't fool God. If what you're doing on the outside doesn't match what's going on inside, you may as well drop the act because God knows it's not real.

The good news is, he can and will change your heart and remake you—if you ask him to. He can make you pure. He can restore your relationship with him.

For more information on God's ability to change your heart, check out Ezekiel 36:24-32.

 ## Random Questions

For decades Ivory Soap has billed itself as being "99 44/100% pure." That begs some questions:

- What's exactly in that other 56/100% that's impure?
- Whose job is it to measure soap impurity?
- What kind of device do you use to measure soap impurities?
- Does each bar of soap contain the same amount of impurity? Or are some bars 99 45/100% pure and others 99 43/100% pure?
- How can you tell when you get to the impure part of the soap?
- Why haven't the Ivory Soap scientists been able to eliminate that last 56/100% of impurity?
- Doesn't that leave the market open for a soap that breaks the 99 44/100% pure barrier?

CPSIA information can be obtained at www.ICGtesting.com
Printed in the USA
LVOW07s1305090414

380939LV00003B/7/P